CIRCULAR WALKS IN THE
BRECON BEACONS NATIONAL PARK

Circular Walks in the Brecon Beacons National Park

Tom Hutton

First edition: 1998
New edition: 2007
© Tom Hutton

ISBN: 1-84524-088-X
978-1-84524-088-2

Cover design: Alan Jones

First published in 1998 by Gwasg Carreg Gwalch
12 Iard yr Orsaf, Llanrwst, Wales LL26 0EH
℡ 01492 642031   📠 01492 641502
✆ books@carreg-gwalch.co.uk   Web site: www.carreg-gwalch.co.uk

New edition published in 2007 by Llygad Gwalch,
Ysgubor Plas, Llwyndyrys, Pwllheli, Gwynedd LL53 6NG
℡ 01758 750432   📠 01758 750438
✆ gai@llygadgwalch.com   Web site: www.carreg-gwalch.co.uk

12 circular walks highlighting the landscape, beauty and history of the Brecon Beacons National Park

Easy to follow directions and maps for all walks and how to get there

Pubs, cafes and local attractions

Information Centres and Youth Hostels

If you want to experience the very best of the Brecon Beacons National Park then this is the book for you. 12 circular walks have been selected to highlight the outstanding beauty and history of the National Park.

There is something for everybody, with short walks suitable for families to big routes to satisfy even the most experienced hillwalker. All routes are easy to follow with clear directions and simple sketch maps. Directions on how to reach the start of each walk are listed, as are details of public transport, where appropriate.

Whether you choose to walk the airy ridges and summits of the highest ground in southern Britain, explore the beautiful valleys, study the varied wildlife or see for yourself the remains of ancient castles and forts, the points of interest will explain what makes each area unique and help you choose the right walk for you and, of course, the conditions! There is a quick reference guide to help you in your choice.

To further entice you there are pubs and cafes, country parks and nature reserves, castles and even a Mountain Information Centre to visit. All Information Centres, Tourist Offices and Youth Hostels are listed. There are also some suggestions for further walks.

Contents

The Walks

The Black Mountains and the Eastern Brecon Beacons (OS maps 1:50 000 Abergavenny and the Black Mountains 161; 1:25 000 Outdoor Leisure 13 The Brecon Beacons National Park Eastern Area)

The Central Brecon Beacons (OS maps 1:50 000 Brecon Beacons 160; 1:25 000 Outdoor Leisure 12 The Brecon Beacons National Park West and Central Area)

Fforest Fach (OS maps 1:50 000 Brecon Beacons 160; 1:25 000 Outdoor Leisure 12 The Brecon Beacons National Park West and Central Area)

Y Mynydd Du (OS maps 1:50 000 Brecon Beacons 160; 1:25 000 Outdoor Leisure 12 The Brecon Beacons National Park West and Central Area)

Features

Other Information

Location Map

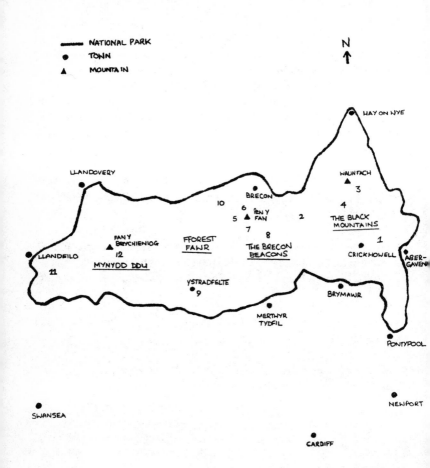

Introduction

It is the author's aim to make this book as easy as possible to follow, whilst offering a varied selection of walks to suit walkers of all ages, levels of fitness and experience. The National Park offers incredible variety. Routes have been chosen carefully so the walker can sample a little of everything on offer. The exact starting point for each walk is given along with simple directions of how to get there. Bus details are given where appropriate but be aware that this is a remote area of narrow country roads and the bus service only really covers the main roads that cross the area. For full details and current timetables check with the Information Centres. Sadly, the best way to explore the National Park is by car. There have, however, been murmurs of a future park and ride service to some of the more remote areas, similar to those operating in other National Parks.

The walks vary in length from 3½ miles/6 kilometres to 12 miles/20 kilometres using mainly public footpaths, bridleways, permissive paths and RUPP's (roads used as public paths). Road walking has been kept to a minimum although it is sometimes necessary to link up the paths. On some of the more strenuous routes which cross open access land, there are sections where no paths exist and good navigational skills are required, particularly in poor visibility. Directions for these sections are clearly explained.

It is difficult to judge how long a walk will take as this will depend heavily on any number of factors including the length of the walk, the fitness of the walker, the amount of ascent and descent and, of course, the weather conditions. The suggested time for each walk is an estimate for a walker of average fitness not allowing for any rest stops. These are included to assist the walker in choosing the appropriate walk and should be used as a rough guide only. It always pays to allow plenty of time, not only to complete the walk safely, but also to enjoy the scenery and points of interest along the way.

A sketch map for each walk is provided, all based upon the 1: 25 000 Ordnance Survey Outdoor Leisure series and the authors observations; they are however, no substitute for the definitive OS (Ordnance Survey) maps themselves. These are available in two formats for the National Park, the 1:50 000 Landranger series show 1.25 inches to a mile (2cm to a kilometre) and cover the National Park in two sheets: Abergavenny and the Black Mountains 161 and The Brecon Beacons 160. These are suitable for most of the walks included, also making it easy to find the start of each walk, showing more than enough detail to navigate around the twisty country lanes. For those who would like more detail there are the Outdoor Leisure Series which offer 2.5 inches to the mile (4cm to the kilometre) and also show field boundaries and more precise details of the landscape. These also cover the Park in two sheets: The Brecon Beacons National Park Eastern Area 13 and The Brecon Beacons National Park West and Central Area 12.

The grading system used is largely self explanatory. The easy walks are considered suitable for all, they will either be fairly short in length where they involve steep ascents or if longer, will be on fairly easy terrain with no major steep climbs or descents. The moderate routes will have a few more steep ascents and descents and, on average, be slightly longer whilst the strenuous routes will involve greater distances, more intricate route finding on more difficult, sometimes pathless terrain with, again, more steep ascents and descents.

Points of interest are included which are designed to give a quick snapshot of a particular area, what gives the walk in landscape, wildlife and history terms, its own brand of uniqueness. They also point out things to look out for along the way. Alternative parking areas are listed under facilities. As the walks are all circular they may be joined at any convenient point and details of the most accessible points are listed. Also included are the nearest public telephones, public toilets, pubs, cafes and shops.

Most small towns and many farms will offer B&B - check with the Information Centres listed for details. A separate list of the Youth Hostels is given in the appendix. Also listed under facilities are any additional places of interest local to the walk e.g. caves, country parks, nature reserves etc.

Mountain Safety

The Brecon Beacons can be very deceptive. The grassy summits and ridges give the area a far more friendly feel than the harder, rocky peaks of other British mountain ranges. Looks can be deceiving. This is the highest ground in Southern Britain and is subject to the same fickle weather systems that all mountains suffer. In summer it may feel hot, calm and sunny in the car park and it would be easy to be tempted to leave jackets and jumpers behind. But the picture can be very different on the summits, for example, on an average summer's day it can be 60°F in the car park. In the sun and out of the wind it will feel very warm indeed. After a long energy sapping climb to 800m the temperature will have dropped a few degrees and you may now be exposed to a strong breeze. 20 mph winds would be considered quite normal at this height and with the wind chill taken into effect the effective temperature now will be near freezing! If, at this stage, some low cloud builds up over the summit which can and does happen fairly frequently on the summit of Pen y Fan, for example, you would now start to get wet. This, at best, would be very uncomfortable and, at worst could lead to the first stages of hypothermia. It is always wise to carry a waterproof jacket and a hat regardless of the weather when you set off.

In winter this can be a harsh mountain environment with temperatures rarely rising above freezing on the summits and frequent snow storms. In these conditions it is best to leave the high places to experienced hill walkers, who will have the equipment and skills to deal with the conditions, and to follow one of the lower level walks.

For maximum comfort a pair of walking boots should be worn on all but the easiest walks. A rucksack is also an advantage for carrying your spare clothing and refreshments. A compass and the knowledge of how to use one is useful in the hills and, in some areas, essential. A simple first aid kit and whistle should also be carried.

On hot days ensure that you carry plenty of water or a soft drink as climbing mountains can be hot work and it is easy to de-hydrate. In cooler weather, a flask of hot tea or coffee can be a great comforter. It is always wise to carry some snacks or sandwiches as your body will quickly burn off energy supplies on a long day in the hills.

In any emergency telephone 999 and ask for Mountain Rescue. It is unwise to rely on mobile telephones in the hills as reception is rarely good. If you do need to use one you may get better reception by climbing to the top of the nearest hills but it's best to not rely on it. If you need to attract help the recognised distress call is six short bursts on a whistle repeated every minute, to respond to a distress call use three short bursts, again, repeated every minute. If you do come across an emergency ensure that the casualty is warm and sheltered, administer any first aid that you are capable of and then go for help. Make a note of exactly where the casualty is (a grid reference would be most useful) and, where possible leave somebody with them.

Always check the weather reports before setting off and advise someone of your route and your estimated time of return. Always remember to inform them when you do return safely. Try to be self sufficient, use common sense and be prepared for any eventuality. Remember that the nearest road may be some miles away. Don't attempt routes which are beyond your skill, experience and fitness level and never be afraid to back off a route early if things go wrong - the mountains will be there another day. Above all, stay safe and enjoy.

The Country Code

Enjoy the country and respect its life and work.
Guard against all risk of fire.
Fasten all gates.
Keep dogs under close control.
Keep to public footpaths across all farmland.
Use gates and stiles to cross field boundaries.
Leave livestock, machinery and crops alone.
Take your litter home.
Help to keep all water clean.
Protect wildlife, plants and trees.
Make no unnecessary noise.

The Brecon Beacons suffer in places from excessive erosion of paths. When walking, try not to add to this erosion by:-

Following any diversions signposted.

Keeping to the main path, trying not to cut corners or make diversions around wet/boggy patches.

Walking in single file on narrow paths to avoid widening them.

Not starting or adding to any cairns.

Remember,

bring only goodwill, leave only footprints, take only photographs and keep only memories.

"We did not inherit the Earth from our parents, we are merely borrowing it from our children."

The Brecon Beacons National Park

The Brecon Beacons National Park was one of ten National Parks set up in the 1950's to conserve the scenery, culture and landscape of some of Britain's most beautiful places. The others are Snowdonia and Pembrokeshire in Wales, whilst England has seven, including the Lake District, Exmoor and Dartmoor. In total, the land covered by these parks covers nearly 10% of the country.

There are now National Parks all over the world with similar aims. Whilst some of these cover mainly wilderness areas, others are lived in and working environments. The Brecon Beacons is very much one of the latter, with people both living and working within its boundaries. Contrary to popular belief the National Park is not publicly owned. In fact, most of the land is actually under private ownership and balancing the needs of the landowners with the needs of the Park is one of the key roles of the National Park Authority.

Ownership of the land (1988)

The National Park Authority	13.7%
Forest Enterprise	8.1%
Welsh Water	6.4%
The National Trust	3.5%

Whilst around 1% of the rest is owned by other bodies such as the MOD and the Nature Conservancy Council it is clear to see that around two thirds of the land is in private ownership.

Use of the land

Cultivation and pasture	39.7%
Common land, moorland & mountains	38.5%
Woodland and forest	13.8%
Reservoirs, buildings, roads, quarries etc.	8.0%

Covering 519 sq. miles (1344 sq. km), the National Park stretches from Llandeilo in the west to Abergavenny in the East and from Hay on Wye in the north to the industrial area of Merthyr Tydfil in the south. It is a land of contrasts, from high peaks and summits to hidden valleys, from open, featureless moorland to rich green pastures and from huge forests to spectacular waterfalls. The Park is made up of four separate Mountain Ranges, each with its own personality. In the east, the Black Mountains rise up from the Usk Valley with huge rounded, peaty summits and miles of open moorland. The central Brecon Beacons, in the heart of the National Park, offer the highest ground with the distinctive table topped summits of Corn Du and Pen y Fan, whilst to their west, the high mountains of Fforest Fawr drop down to the spectacular waterfalls and forests around Ystradfellte. On the western extremities are the Mynydd Du or Black Mountain (singular). This is a wild landscape with huge steep escarpments and spectacular limestone outcrops, all relatively untouched by man.

The National Park is run by a National Park Authority who's job it is to balance the needs of the landscape and environment with the demands of both visitors and local people. It offers specialist advice on conservation, wildlife, woodlands and buildings and sets up management agreements with farmers and landowners in order to protect the environment and culture of the area. It is also responsible for providing the Parks visitors with education and information as well as managing funds and grants and maintaining the public rights of way network.

Most of the estimated seven million visits per year to the National Park are made by day visitors with only a third made by holiday makers staying one night or more. This leads to the conclusion that the Park attracts more people from South Wales and the local area than from further afield. Amongst the many attractions bringing these visitors to the park are walking, cycling, caving, canoeing, pony trekking and fishing. Other sightseeing attractions including castles, churches, a variety of arts and crafts and many picnic areas that offer something of interest for the less energetic.

The National Park is not, as often thought, a nature reserve but there are many nature reserves within its boundaries. These cover high mountains, woodlands, lakes, rivers and even the only cave reserve in Britain, Ogof Ffynnon Ddu. They are home to a wide variety of birds, mammals, plants and insects, some of them rare.

Rights of way and public access in the National Park

Over a third of the land within the National Park is common land and walkers can enjoy great freedom, roaming almost at will around these areas. It is, however, important to understand that there is **no** public right of access to this land, except for public rights of way or places open to the public by law.

The freedom to roam in these hills is based on the tradition of *de facto* access that is established in the area. The National Park Authority acts as a guardian to this tradition and would defend any attempt to challenge it.

The National Trust, who own much of the high land in the Central Brecon Beacons as well as the Sugar Loaf in the Black Mountains, is required by law to allow the public onto its common land and therefore has a key role to play in this important issue.

The History of the Landscape

Whilst it would be ideal to describe the landscape and its formation separately from the history of man in the Park, the two are inextricably linked making the landscape a fascinating mix of natural processes and the influence of man and his activities.

The shape of the landscape is largely influenced by its rock. There are three main types in the park. Each type has its own corresponding scenery and characteristics, yet all were formed from sediment. Starting life as sand and gravel on the floors of great oceans they would have been slowly compressed over millions of years into hard rock. The activities of giant forces deep within the Earth's crust then lifted and tilted the layers into hills and mountains. These hills and mountains would then have been altered by glacial action at the end of the last Ice Age, with the retreating ice grinding away the rock formations to form the wide U-shaped valleys and characteristic north facing escarpments that we see today. Over thousands of years rocks and sediments deposited by the glaciers have weathered and crumbled to produce fertile soils which, in turn, have encouraged the farming of the landscape, further altering its shape.

Predominant across all four mountain ranges is Old Red

Sandstone. The mountains are capped with a hard layer of tough conglomerates and sandstones known as the Plateau Beds. These are responsible for the table top shape of many of the mountains and ridges. The spectacular, steep escarpments and rocky ledges found all over the Park are all made up of this type of rock.

In sharp contrast is the Millstone Grit found mainly in the Fforest Fawr area around Ystradfellte. As the mountain streams plunge down from the hills they have worn away the softer rock beds and now plummet over hard rock ledges to create huge waterfalls, the highest of these being nearly 30 metres tall.

Scattered throughout the Park are areas of carboniferous limestone. This gives a landscape of rocky outcrops, crags, cliffs and strange, almost man made pavements. Soluble in nature, the limestone has dissolved and worn away over thousands of years to create underground rivers and cave systems such as Ogof Ffynnon Ddu in the Black Mountain which is one of the longest in Europe. On the surface the action of slightly acidic rain dissolves the rock as it drips through cracks further altering the landscape as the cave roofs partially collapse creating crater-like shake and swallow holes.

Man's influence on the landscape is predominantly linked to farming. The first settlers in the area would have started clearing the primeval forest to grow crops and rear livestock over 5000 years ago. Nowadays there are almost a million sheep within the Park! (an average of 30 sheep for every person living there.) Whilst the landscape may look wild and natural, the activities of man and his livestock have affected all of the countryside as we know it today. The Industrial Revolution also played its part, particularly in the south where all the raw materials needed to produce iron could be found. Coal mines, quarries and, of course, iron works started up and a transport infrastructure was created based around the Monmouthshire and Brecon canal.

More recently man's influence has been to directly reshape the landscape with the creation of 19 reservoirs, huge coniferous forests and, of course, roads, houses and other buildings. We must hope that in the capable hands of the National Park Authority, man's effect on the landscape will be less marked in the future.

People in the Park

People first came to the area over 5,000 years ago. The earliest visitors were most likely Mesolithic hunter-gatherers who would have hunted and lived in a very different environment to the one we know now. The tree line would have been at about 2,000 ft, below which would have been dense forests of pine, birch and oak throughout. The area would have been inhabited by deer, wild oxen, wolves and bears, whilst the weather would have been a lot warmer than it is now.

The first true settlers in the area were probably New Stone Age people who would have lived in wood houses. These people would have started to clear the forests to grow crops and to graze livestock. Over centuries, as the land became exhausted from continual agriculture, they cleared more and more forest and the hills became covered with scrub and heathland. These Neolithic people buried their dead in communal tombs – large, chambered cairns, the remains of which can be seen in a few places in the National Park.

Next came continental visitors to the area, bringing hand crafted tools and metal-making skills. Now able to use tools to cultivate the land, development accelerated into the start of the Bronze Age. These people left many more signs of their civilisation than their predecessors and the area is littered with standing stones including the remarkable example of Maen Llia in Fforest Fawr. There are also many stone circles and most notably, circular stone cairns, where they would have buried their dead. Examples of these have been found and excavated on many of the Parks highest peaks including Corn Du and Pen y Fan.

The weather in the area would have started to get colder as the Iron Age approached and this, plus improved tools, would have allowed the people to build bigger, more permanent settlements. It was around this time that the first hill forts started to appear. These were not military style fortifications but villages that could be easily defended from attack. They would have worked much as society does today with a social and political structure. There are over 20 of these hill forts within the park with the best example being on Garn Goch common which is one of the largest in Wales and still has the remains of stone wall ramparts. It is thought that the Bronze Age people are responsible for the origins of the Welsh language as they introduced Celtic into Britain, which then evolved into Welsh, Gaelic and Cornish.

When the Romans invaded Wales at the end of the Iron Age they swept into the country from the east but found it difficult to gain any foothold in the area of the Park. They did eventually conquer and built forts and the roads which linked them together. A fine example of a Roman Military Fort is Y Gaer near Brecon. Here it is still possible to see stone walls and foundations. The best example of a Roman Road in the Park is Sarn Helen which linked Y Gaer to Coelbren Fort further south. During the fifth and sixth centuries Christianity started to take hold in Wales, brought in by Celtic missionaries who traveled in the area spreading the word of Christ.

There then followed a bloodthirsty period of unrest, as the Normans started almost two hundred years of fighting and feuding with the Welsh Lords. Starting in the east, like the Romans many years before them, the Normans moved westwards across South Wales, fighting long and bloody battles for each territory gained along the way. Having established a territory, they then built castles in strategic placements. Good examples of these can be seen at Trecastle, Crickhowell and Brecon.

By the fifteenth century more peaceful times had returned to the area and there were no major developments in the history of the area until the seventeenth century and the beginning of the Industrial Revolution. Few places would have seen such marked effects of this period as the south eastern fringes of the Park. Here in abundance were all the raw materials to make Iron, whilst the rivers were utilised to power machinery and mills. Later, as coal was discovered, the area became heavily mined. This is something which has had a large influence in the social development of South Wales to this day. With all this industry, a transport network was required to move both raw materials and finished product. Many tramways and roads were built, linking this production to the Monmouthshire and Brecon canal. This was used in the early nineteenth century as the main form of transport between Brecon and Newport. By the end of that century railways had taken over and the canal became redundant.

This century has seen the plantation of forests, the creation of reservoirs and, perhaps the most influential development in the Park today, the advent of tourism. The management of this will surely be one of the biggest challenges for the National Park Authority as we head for the Millennium.

Wildlife in the Park

One of the great attractions of this area is its wide variety of wildlife. Whilst it is beyond the remit of this book to offer a comprehensive guide to the wildlife, it would be a serious omission if it wasn't mentioned at all.

At first sight the high moors and mountains of the Park appear baron with no obvious signs of life aside from the sheep and wild horses. A closer look will reveal that this is far from the truth. Most of the moorland is covered with tough grasses but in places heather, billberry and gorse grow, giving a bright, colourful Autumn vista. Alpine plants such as purple saxifrage grow in some areas, a remnant of the last Ice Age.

There are many birds in these areas, with ravens, buzzards and kestrel all commonplace, and other raptors including rare peregrine falcons, hobbies, merlins and the red kite; probably the most beautiful of all our native birds. Closer to the ground, look for skylark, pipits, wheatear and even waders and grouse in the autumn and winter. This is a hostile environment for mammals but even so, it's always quite exciting to catch the site of the odd fox, again proving its ability to adapt to almost any habitat.

The lakes and rivers in the National Park are home to many species of bird and mammal. Dippers and wagtails frequent most of the streams sharing some locations with herons and kingfisher. The lakes are an important winter refuge for many migrating birds. Otters seem to be enjoying something of a revival in the area and there is an ever increasing population of mink.

The lowland areas of woodland and farmland provide ideal habitats for a number of different creatures. Insects, small birds and mammals provide prey for owls and sparrowhawks. The trees themselves can be literally teeming with birdlife. Treecreepers and nuthatches share the tree trunks with woodpeckers. Many species of the tit family can be seen, as can flycatchers, jays and even the diminutive goldcrest. In spring many of the woodlands come alive with colour, as bluebells and primrose carpet the forest floor. Later in the year the colours come from toadstools and mushrooms in the shade of the trees and from the stunning yellow gorse at the edge of the mountain ranges.

The Park is unlikely to disappoint the observant nature lover armed with a good pair of binoculars.

Welsh Place Names

Great satisfaction can be gained from a small understanding of the names of the places that you visit. Most place names are simply descriptions in the Welsh language of the features of the area. After a while many of these become familiar, giving clues as to what to expect when you arrive. The following list, whilst by no means definitive, covers some of the more commonly used words and phrases.

Aber – confluence, usually a river mouth.
Afon – river
Allt (Gallt) – hill, usually wooded
Bach (Fach, Bychan) – small
Bedd – grave
Betws – chapel
Blaen – head of valley, source
Bont – bridge
Braich – arm
Bwlch – pass
Cadair – chair
Caer – fort
Capel – chapel
Carn (Carnedd) – a pile of stones
Carreg – stone
Castell – castle

Cau – deep hollow
Cefn – ridge
Clogwyn – cliff
Coch (Goch) – red
Coed – wood
Craig – crag
Crib – narrow ridge
Cwm – mountain valley
Dinas – town or hill fort
Du (Ddu) – black
Dŵr – water
Dyffryn – valley
Eglwys – church
Eira – snow
Esgair – long ridge
Ffordd – road, path

21

Ffynnon – well, spring	*Ogof* – cave
Glas (Las) – blue-green	*Pant* – small hollow
Gribin – jagged ridge	*Pen* – peak
Gwyllt – wild	*Pistyll* – waterfall or waterspout
Gwyn – white	*Pont* – bridge
Gwynt – wind	*Porth* – gate or door
Hafod – summer dwelling	*Pwll* – pool
Hen – old	*Rhaeadr* – waterfall
Hendre – winter dwelling	*Rhyd* – ford
Hir – long ridge	*Saeth* – arrow
Isaf – lower	*Sarn* – causeway
Llech – flat stone	*Sych* – dry
Llethr – slope	*Tref* – town
Llithrig – slippery	*Twll* – hole
Llyn – lake	*Tŷ* – house
Maen – stone	*Uchaf* – highest
Mawr (Fawr) – big	*Waun* – moor
Moel (Foel) – rounded hill	*Wen (Gwyn)* – white
Mynydd (Fynydd) – mountain	*Y (Yr)* – the, of the
Nant – stream or brook	*Ynys* – island
Newydd – new	*Ysgol* – ladder

Quick Reference Guide

If you are looking for a particular type of walk e.g. strenuous high mountain walks, or are interested in a particular subject e.g. castles or hill forts, then the following quick reference guide is given. The list is not exhaustive and only the principle types or sites are given.

Easy Walks
High Mountains ; **1,5.**
Riverside ; **9,11.**
Woodlands ; **2, 9,11.**
Hill Forts/Historical ; **2,10,11.**
Memorials ; **5.**

Moderate Walks
High Mountains ; **3, 6,7,8.**
Riverside ; **3, 6,8.**
Woodlands ;
Memorials; **6,8.**

Strenuous Walks
High Mountains ; **4,12.**
Riverside; **4,12.**

Information

Tourist Information Centres

Abergavenny - Swan Meadow, Cross Street.	Tel : 01873 857588
Brecon- Cattle Market Car Park.	Tel : 01874 62485
Builth Wells - The Groe Car Park.	Tel : 01982 553307
Crickhowell - Beaufort Chambers, Beaufort St.	Tel : 01873 812105
Hay on Wye - Craft Centre, Oxford Road.	Tel : 01497 820144
Llandovery - Heritage Centre, Kings Road.	Tel : 01550 720693
Merthyr Tydfil - 14a Glebeland Street.	Tel : 01685 379884
Pontneddfechan - Nr Glynneath.	Tel : 01639 721795

Brecon Beacons National Park Centres

Headquarters - 7 Glamorgan Street, Brecon, Powys. LD3 7DP
> Tel: 01874 624437
> Fax: 01874 622574

National Park Visitor Centre (Mountain Centre) Libanus, Nr Brecon. Powys. LD3 8ER
> Tel: 01874 623366
> Fax: 01874 624515

Abergavenny - Swan Meadow, Cross Street.
> Tel: 01873 857588

Craig-y-nos Country Park - Brecon Road, Pen y Cae, Swansea Valley, SA9 1GL
> Tel: 01639 730395
> Fax: 01639 730395

Llandovery - Heritage Centre, Kings Road, Llandovery.
> Tel: 01550 720693

Public Transport

Bus Services:
Stagecoach :   01633 266336
Silverline :   01874 623900
Note: These are very rural areas, Bus services can be infrequent. Consult timetables before leaving.

Railway Services:
The nearest railway stations are at Abergavenny and Merthyr Tydfil, which both link with the Paddington to South Wales line. Also close by are Llandeilo and Llandovery, which are both on the Heart of Wales line.

Weather services
Weather Call : South Wales 0891 500409

More Walks
Offa's Dyke
A long distance footpath which runs from Chepstow in the south-east to Prestatyn in the north. This fine route crosses the Brecon Beacons in the Black Mountains where it could easily be followed in either a linear format or incorporated into a circular walk around Hay Bluff.

The Taff Trail
This is a fascinating long distance route which loosely follows the route of the River Taff running from Cardiff to Brecon. It runs through the heart of the National Park close to Pen y Fan and the central Brecon Beacons and whilst offering a great insight into the area doesn't involve strenuous climbs and descents. For further information: The Taff Trail Project, Groundwork Mertyr and Cynon, Fedw Hir, Llwytcoed, Aberdare CF44 0DX. 01685 883880.

The Usk Valley Walk
This route follows the towpath of the Monmouthshire and Brecon Canal and runs through the National Park.

Other Forest Walks
Much of the wooded land within the National Park is owned by the

Forest Enterprise and there are many short walks signposted in some of these which would be suitable for a gentle stroll for the family.

Guided Walks

The Park Service organises a number of guided walks around the National Park. Details of the programme can be obtained from the information centres listed.

Other Attractions

There are, of course, many other attractions in the National Park that fall outside of the walks included, where these are situated near the walks, details have been included in the facilities section. Some of the other attractions also well worth a visit are listed below.

Garwnant Forest Centre (Cwm Taf-6 miles north of Merthyr Tydfil)
An exhibition of the work of the Forest Enterprise plus picnic areas and well marked forest walks. (01685 723060)

Big Pit (Blaenavon - 6 miles south west of Abergavenny)
This was a working colliery until 1980. It now offers visitors underground tours and displays of mining life. (01495 790311)

Blaenavon Iron Works (Blaenavon - 6 miles south west of Abergavenny)
The best preserved display of the Industrial Revolution and its effects on South Wales. (01495 792615)

Trefeinon Open Farm (B4560 between Talgarth and Llan-gors)
Deer herds and breeding horses. (01874 658607)

Mountain Railway (Pant Station, Dowlais. 2 miles north of Merthyr Tydfil)
A narrow gauge steam train which runs on a very scenic route into the National Park. (01685 384854)

There are many other displays and museums, for further details see the Information Centres listed.

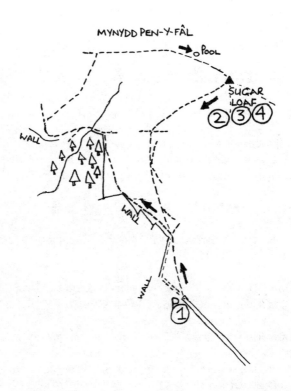

The Sugar Loaf

A fairly gentle hill walk with spectacular panoramic views of the Black Mountains.

OS maps :	1:50 000 Abergavenny and The Black Mountains 161. 1:25 000 Outdoor Leisure 13, The Brecon Beacons National Park Eastern Area.
Start:	National Trust Car Park just off the A40, 2 kilometres west of Abergavenny. GR 268167
Access:	By car, follow the A40 West from Abergavenny. Turn right immediately after leaving the built up area. Follow the signs to Sugar Loaf.
Grade:	Easy - The route follows good, clear paths over open moorland. There are many tracks that could be used to return to the car park, should the weather deteriorate. The climbing is fairly gentle with a short steep push to reach the summit.

Points of Interest:

1. At 345 metres above sea level, the views probably make this the most visited car park in the National Park. The information board provided by the Automobile Association outlines the main points of interest, including the summits of nearby Blorenge, Mynydd Llangatwg and the more distant Waen Rhyd. Be warned, this is not an area of solitude or wilderness. On a hot summer's afternoon, many people will make the drive to this car park and enjoy a picnic here, walking only a few yards from the car. This is one of the few places you will see the usually hardened mountain sheep happily take tit-bits from your hand.

From here you will notice that there are many paths leading directly to the summit and back. It is possible to take one of these and shorten the days walking by almost 2 miles. These paths, however, fail to offer the walker the real mountain experience and quite stunning views of the Black Mountains that this route offers.

2. If Pen y Fan is the most climbed mountain in the central Brecon Beacons then the Sugar Loaf must be the most popular in the eastern range. It lies on the Eastern extremities of the National Park and is isolated from the main Black Mountains by the Vale of Grwyne. From the summit, this isolation allows superb views in all directions. The peaks of the central Brecon Beacons can be clearly seen in the distance whilst closer to you the main range of the Black Mountains unfolds. In front of you, you will see the unique Table Mountain tucked neatly in the shadow of the impressive summit ridge of Pen Cerrig Calch. This is the western flank of a horseshoe shaped glacial valley. At the head of the valley is Waun Fach (the small moor), which at 811m, is the highest point of the Black Mountains. Unfortunately, due to its almost flat summit, it doesn't look anything like as impressive as its near neighbour Pen y Gadair Fawr which, although 11 metres smaller, has a more conical peak. (These hills are themselves the subject of another walk in this book.)

To the east you will see Skirrid Mountain, in Welsh, Ysgyryd Fawr. This truly is the easternmost hill in the National Park and, whilst not as high as the Sugar Loaf, has a much more wild feel. Often referred to as the Holy Mountain, its slopes are home to the remains of a medieval chapel. It is well worth exploring in its own right.

3. To the south east you can see the town of Abergavenny. Although often referred to as the eastern gateway to the National Park, it actually lies just outside of the boundary. The town is named after the confluence (Aber) of the Gavenny stream with the river Usk and makes a great base for exploring the eastern hills. Once fortified by the Normans, it is today a bustling market town boasting many attractions including a fascinating museum. Housed in a rebuilt section of its twelfth century castle, displays of local history, archaeology and industry can all be seen. Also worth a visit is the church, which,

amongst others, contains the tombs of members of the infamous de Braose family. William de Braose once held the castle in the town for a short period and was renowned for his cruelty to the local people.

4. The summit of the Sugar Loaf has to be the best place in the National Park for watching Ravens. Although they inhabit most of the area, they always seem to be present here. Watch their superb arial displays as they rise effortlessly on updraughts before making spectacular plummeting dives. Growing to over two feet long with a huge wingspan, on first impressions these birds appear to be no more than large crows. They are, however, true masters of flight and it is easy to while away a brief rest-stop marveling at their antics. If you are lucky enough to get close, you will see quite clearly their huge beaks and hear their strange 'gronk' call. In common with most of the mountains in the National Park, this is a good place to see meadow pipits, wheatears, sky larks and even an occasional buzzard or kestrel.

Walk Directions: (-) denotes point of interest.

Note: This area is criss-crossed with paths running in all directions and it is not advisable to attempt this walk in poor visibility unless you are skilled at using a map and a compass.

1. From the far end of the car park (1), take the path which heads slightly uphill in a northwesterly direction. Follow this gentle rise for approximately half a kilometre until you reach the corner of a dry stone wall on your left.

2. At the wall, there is effectively a crossroads. Go straight across the crossroads keeping roughly parallel with the wall. After 200 metres, there is a fork in the path, keep left here and again 400 metres further on where you will meet another fork. The wall should remain on your left at all times.

3. The path will start to go downhill and you will see a wood to your left in the valley below. At this stage the path leaves the wall and heads towards the far corner of this wood, now dropping quite steeply.

4. At the corner of the wood, the path is joined by another from the right. Carry straight on here and descend steeply to a small stream.

5. Cross the stream, ignoring the path which turns immediately left, down the valley. Instead, carry straight on along the main track, climbing directly up the hill in front of you, then trending leftwards nearer the top. After 200 metres you will meet a field boundary on your left.

6. As the path begins to level out, it curves quite sharply to the right. Just after this, as it starts to straighten again, take the wide track to your right and start walking uphill.

7. Carry on to the top of the ridge where another path comes in from the left. Turn right at this junction and follow the ridge. This will take you all the way to the summit of Sugar Loaf (2,3,4).

8. From the summit you will see the criss-cross of paths described earlier in the walk directions. Once you are fully rested, turn right at the trig point and follow the path which heads steeply down hill in a westerly direction. This curves round towards the left (south) as it drops.

9. Ignore one major crossroads then, after 400 metres, fork right at another. Staying on this path, you will be heading in a southeasterly direction until you once again meet a dry stone wall. This is the wall you followed at the start of the walk.

10.Turn left, and this time with the wall on your right, retrace your footsteps for the remaining half a kilometre or so, back to the car park.

Facilities

The car park is fairly isolated. There are pubs, shops and public telephones in Abergavenny.

Walk 2   *4 miles/6 kilometres*
                                            2-3 hours

Allt yr Esgair

A delightful woodland stroll with wide reaching views, a Roman road and ancient earthworks.

OS maps: 1:50 000 Abergavenny and The Black Mountains 161:
                1:25 000 Outdoor Leisure 13, The Brecon Beacons
                National Park Eastern area.

Start: Car park and public conveniences on the A40,
                2 kilometres north west of Bwlch. GR129227.

Access: By car follow the A40 West from Crickhowell through
                the village of Bwlch. Approximately 2 kilometres
                further on there is a large lay-by on the right. The route
                could also be reached by the No. 21 bus service which
                runs between Brecon and Newport.

Grade: Easy - The route follows good clear paths through
                woodland to hilltop. The climbing is always very gentle.

Points of Interest:

1. The woodland itself is very varied with ancient trees now surrounded by more recent plantings. In addition to the splendor of the huge oak and beech trees you will see hazel groves, birch and scots pine. There is now a tree planting project in existence in the National Park. Old dead trees being replaced by new ones which, once planted, are generally fenced off to protect them from grazing sheep. The natural regeneration of the woodland has been prevented in the recent past by grazing animals. This has led to these measures being taken in order to preserve this fascinating and important habitat.

Sadly you will also see a number of dead, decaying trees. These are elm trees that fell victim to the dreadful Dutch elm disease.

31

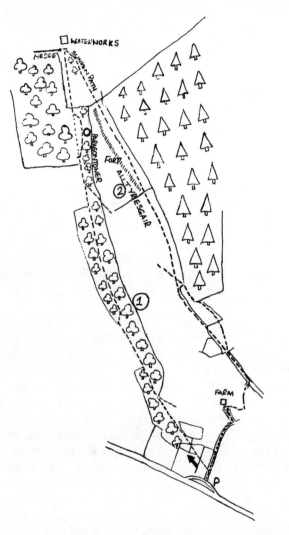

N

WATERWORKS

HEDGE

Sunken Path

WATER TOWER

FORD

ALLT-YRESGAIR

②

①

FARM

P

A40

The woodland supports a wide variety of wildlife. Most commonly seen will be blue tits, great tits, robins, blackbirds and woodpigeon. Keep your eyes open for squirrels as they dive for cover upon your arrival. In Autumn the woodland is home to many mushrooms and toadstools. These are a fascinating subject in their own right and add colour and interest to the woodland floor.

At the far end of the woods is a ruined 19th century hunting lodge, the Paragon Tower.

The circular main building boasts a huge central chimney which is shared by the four quadrant shaped rooms that surround it.

2. Once gained, the ridge after which the area is named (Allt yr Esgair translates to the ridge of the hill) gives outstanding views to both the central Brecon Beacons and the Black Mountains. To the west, the peaks of Pen y Fan and Cribyn can be seen whilst to the east the valleys open out between Pen Tir and Mynydd Llangorse.

A lot closer, the Usk valley can be seen. The river Usk winds lazily past Talybont from its source on the western side of the National Park near the Mynydd Du. The river runs almost the complete width of the National Park and is home to fine game fish as well as many other creatures including the eye-catching kingfisher and the illusive otter. This shy creature is currently making a comeback in the area but is seldom seen unless you are particularly lucky.

Also in full view now is Llangorse Lake, a vitally important wetland habitat which is coming under increasing pressure from recreational use. It is the largest naturally formed lake in South Wales which, like many mountain lakes, is a result of the receding glaciers at the end of the Ice Age. (See Llyn Cwm Llwch in walk 6) It is now home to flora and fauna of all types including eels and fish. It also provides a winter refuge for many wildfowl. The effects of watersports and farming on the lake are currently being carefully monitored by the National Park Authority to ensure the future protection of the wildlife that depend upon it.

On the grassy summit of the ridge lie the remains of an ancient earthworks. These, along with the sunken paths give the whole area a very historic feel.

Walk Directions:

1. From the lay-by, walk through a gate and up the shaded footpath. Almost immediately, go left through another gate and into a field. Cross the field diagonally uphill, through yet another gate and fork right at the top to enter the woodland (1).

2. After a few hundred meters you will be joined by a path from the left. Turn left here and continue on, making steady progress uphill.

3. At the next fork keep to the right, before passing through several gates along the track. All the time you will continue to make progress up the hill.

4. You will come to a small gate where the path forks again. Keep to the right here and after a few minutes you will come to the ruined buildings of the Paragon Tower.

5. Having explored the ruins continue on along the path, in a short while it will drop slightly down hill and join up with the path that you chose not to take at the last gate. Turn right onto this path and shortly afterwards you will leave the woodland and enter a grassy hillside pasture.

6. Cross the field by the faint path which traverses the hillside, neither gaining or losing height and aim towards the hedge at the far end of the field. Once you get near to the hedge you will see some waterworks buildings. Aim towards these until you come to a gate. Here you turn sharply back on yourself (right) and start to climb up the main ridge by either the main sunken path or, to its right and running parallel to it, another less claustrophobic path. On your left will be a dry stone wall.

7. Carry on up the hill following the dry stone wall and ignoring a path on your right, until you reach the grassy summit of Allt yr Esgair, guarded by small but impressive rocky crags (2).

8. After taking in the views, carry on along the path, keeping the wall to your left. Beyond the wall your view will be spoiled by a large conifer plantation.

9. You will pass a full size gate on your left before coming to a smaller gate which you pass through into a field. Follow the path along the top of the field with the wall on your right this time. You will see a ruined building down to your left.

10. At the other side of the field you will arrive at a shady, straight lane between two hedgerows. This is in fact, an old roman road, which carries on towards the village of Bwlch. Unless you fancy a few extra miles, leave this lane shortly, turning right through a gate into another shady lane. Walk steeply down hill until you reach a farm.

11. At the farm, turn sharply left and then sharply right. This is now the lane you started on. Follow it down hill to the lay-by.

Facilities

As well as public conveniences there is often a snack van in the lay-by during the summer months.

There are picnic tables in the lay-by at the start and finish of the walk.

Public telephones can be found at Talybont on Usk and Bwlch where a selection of shops and pubs can also be found.

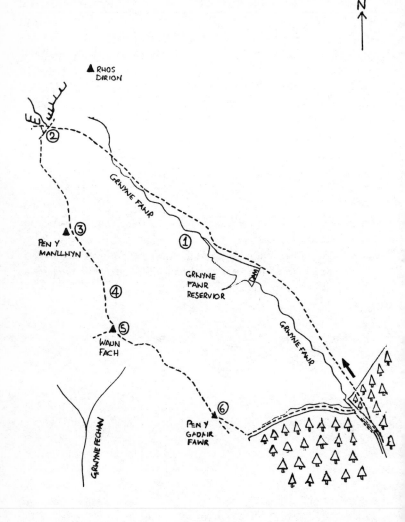

N

▲ RHOS DIRION

GRWYNE FAWR

② ③ PEN Y MANLLHYN

④

⑤ WAUN FACH

① GRWYNE FAWR RESERVIOR

DAM

GRWYNE FAWR

⑥ PEN Y GADAIR FAWR

GRWYNE FECHAN

Grwyne Fawr - Waun Fach

A great introduction to the Black Mountains including the highest point Waun Fach and great views in all directions.

OS map :	1:50 000 Abergavenny and the Black Mountains 161: 1:25 000 Outdoor Leisure 13, The Brecon Beacons National Park Eastern area
Start:	Car Park and picnic area at Blaen-y-cwm at the end of the minor road north of the Forest Coal Pit. Approximately 10km north of Abergavenny. GR253284.
Access:	By car, from Abergavenny or Crickhowell follow minor roads towards the Forest Coal Pit. (Signposted). From the five way junction by a telephone box, head north along the side of the Grwyne Fawr river to the end of the road.
Grade:	Moderate - Mainly clear paths over open moorland. The climbs, although quite long are reasonably easy. In damp weather it can be boggy in places.

Points of Interest:

1. The first few kilometres of the walk follow the Grwyne Fawr river to the Grwyne Fawr reservoir. Above the reservoir, the river becomes a typical mountain stream as it meanders down from the hills above. Along the way it is joined by many steep sided gorges from the west, most of which are fairly craggy and contain delightful hanging gardens of ferns, mosses and lichen. There are many small waterfalls and rapids which make great places to stop for a rest. Look out for dippers in the stream and herons who occupy the banks, searching for fish.

2. At the head of the valley the path meets the northern escarpment of the Black Mountains. From here there are views in all directions. To

the north is Hay on Wye, and to the northwest, the summit of Rhos Dirion which obscures Twmpa and Hay Bluff. The peaks of the Central Brecon Beacons can be seen to the west.

3. As you climb up towards Waun Fach you can clearly see to your west, the isolated hill of Mynydd Troed. Beyond this, the distinctive table top summit of Pen y Fan can be seen in the central Brecon Beacons and, in the far distance, the shapely escarpment of the Mynydd Du on the far western edge of the Park.

4. The path on this stretch is broken up by peat hags. These strange, almost mushroom shaped trenches are found in many parts of the National Park. Peat is formed where vegetable matter has decayed and broken down in a very wet atmosphere - something that this area undoubtedly had! Starved of oxygen, the bacteria that would normally cause this matter to rot away cannot exist. Therefore, instead of rotting completely, a jelly like substance is formed. In some areas of South Wales this jelly would have been pressurised by rock layers above, forming coal. Where there is no rock layer above it forms bogs which can be seen all over the National Park. These bogs gradually dry out over thousands of years and are easily weathered by the extremities of the mountain climate. Running water from rain, ice and snow combine with frosts and high winds to erode trenches and ruts in the peat. These ruts can be four or five foot deep in places. This is the type of peat that, in some areas, is cut into huge slabs for fuel or for use as a garden fertilizer. There is however, no history of peat cutting in this area so the patterns we see are all created naturally. Although spectacular, it can be difficult to walk in these areas, particularly after long damp spells.

5. Waun Fach, translated into Welsh, means the little moor. At 811m it is the highest point of the Black Mountains and is a popular target for hill walkers, even though it doesn't really have a summit, just a flat stone laid in a boggy area of peat.

6. To the south east, the summit of Pen y Gadair Fawr, although eleven metres lower, actually looks higher than Waun Fach due to its more sharply defined peak on which is found a large, perfectly formed cairn. Here you have superb views over the Black Mountains and, in

particular, the valley of Grwyne Fechan which now opens up in front of you. This valley is the subject of another walk in this book.

Walk Directions: (-) denotes point of interest.

1. From the car park, continue on up the road to a stony path on the right. Take this path and follow it up to the reservoir (1). Continue on past the reservoir over wide open moorland until you finally cross the Grwyne Fawr river.

2. After the crossing, the path veers slightly more westerly and after another 500 metres, joins up with a number of other paths at the edge of the escarpment (2).

3. Having stopped to enjoy the views, take the path which heads across the plateau to your left. Turn left again after a few hundred metres and you will now be heading due south towards Waun Fach. Follow this path over two small climbs (3) to the summit stone (4) (5).

4. From the summit stone follow the path to your left (south east) over boggy ground. At first you will drop slightly, then doing your best to follow the path over the flat, peaty plateau, climb in 3 stages to the summit cairn of Pen y Gadair Fawr (6).

5. From the cairn, continue along this path for a further 100 metres before following a lesser path as it forks left towards the top corner of a wood. When you reach the wood you will see a path heading steeply downhill along the side of the fence. Take this path, keeping close to the fence and taking care not to slip if the ground is wet.

6. Carry on down the path with the woods on your right and a small stream to your left. Although narrow and tricky in places, this path will eventually bring you out on the banks of the Grwyne Fawr.

7. Turn right along the side of the river to a footbridge. Cross the footbridge and turn right onto the road back to the car park.

Facilities

This is an isolated area and you will need to be self sufficient. There is however, a public telephone 500 metres down the road at Coed Dinas.

Near the start of the walk is the delightful hamlet of Llanthony and the ruins of the 13th Century Llanthony Priory.

The Offa's Dyke National Trail runs close to the Grwyne Fawr Reservoir and could be linked in with this route if you fancied a much longer walk.

Table Mountain - Pen Allt-mawr
- Grwyne Fechan

A strenuous yet highly rewarding horseshoe exploring the quieter parts of the Black Mountains and a charming valley.

OS maps:	1:50 000 Abergavenny and the Black Mountains 161: 1:25 000 Outdoor Leisure 13, The Brecon Beacons National Park Eastern area
Start:	Small lay-by on the minor road north from Crickhowell past Llanbedr. GR234228.
Access:	By car, from Crickhowell follow the minor road north towards Llanbedr. Where the road forks right to the village, carry straight on until it dips down a steep hill with a tight right hand bend at the bottom. The lay-by is a few metres after the bend on the left.
Grade:	Strenuous - This is a long and demanding walk over high mountains. It generally follows good clear paths so navigation should prove fairly straightforward.

Points of Interest:

1. As you follow the path along the side of the wood and then the wall which separates the open moor from the pastures below, keep an eye open for the many species of small bird that frequent this type of habitat. Many members of the acrobatic tit family can be seen flitting around in the trees as well as the diminutive little wren which can nest in the dry stone wall. On occasions, the magical goldcrest will be spotted skipping around in the bracken on the moors edge or in the trees. By standing still and keeping quiet it is possible to watch these little entertainers for an age. They are Europe's smallest birds at

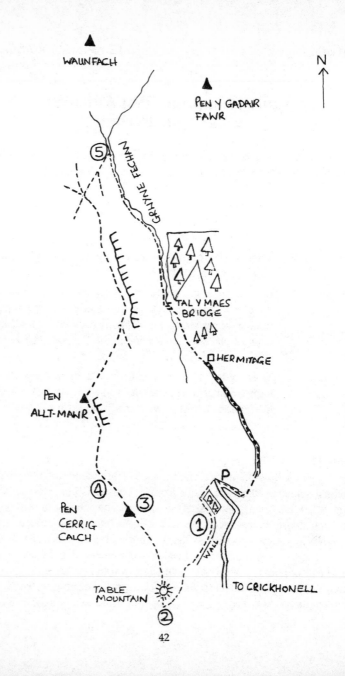

WAUNFACH

N

PEN Y GADAIR
FAWR

⑤

GRWYNE FECHAN

TAL Y MAES
BRIDGE

☐ HERMITAGE

PEN
ALLT-MAWR

P

④ ③

PEN
CERRIG
CALCH

①

WALL

TABLE
MOUNTAIN

② TO CRICKHONELL

around 8cm from tip to tail, and are easily recognised by their size and by their bright golden crest. Their very high pitched call resembles the ringing of a fairy bell and makes spotting them really quite enchanting.

2. Table Mountain is a fine example of a hill fort perched high above the town of Crickhowell (or Crug Hywel) to which it lends its name. Its position, which would have offered incredible defences to its inhabitants, now offers wide views of the Usk Valley to scores of walkers who ascend to its summit. Despite looking flat on top from below it is surprisingly sloping once upon it. The forts naturally defensive position was strengthened with ramparts all round. Generally, there are two of these but in the weaker areas there are four. Probably constructed at the end of the Iron Age, the fort derives its name from King Hywel (literally, Crug Hywel, Hywel's Fort) who was a tenth century Welsh King. Hywel is often referred to as the man who united Wales. He did, in fact, manage to unite Gwynedd, Powys and Dyfed over which, during his rule, he became known as Hywel Dda (*Hywel the Good*). He failed, however, to add Gwent and Glamorgan to his kingdom therefore the legend isn't strictly true. He earned his name of "the Good" by passing many laws giving increased rights to his subjects. These included some forward thinking equal rights for women, as well as a series of definitions designed to ensure that the common man didn't live forever at the mercy of merchants. These definitions laid out everything from specifications for gold plates to the value of domestic cats that could catch mice.

Strangely, the Norman invaders chose not to build their castle up here on the hill. Perhaps it would have been a little tight for space! They instead built a fine castle in the town itself. Its ruins can still be visited.

3. The next stop after Table Mountain will be the summit of Pen Cerrig Calch which is adorned with a concrete triangulation pillar. Pen Cerrig Calch translates into the "Peak of the limestone rocks or limestone top" which accurately describes this small oasis of limestone in a huge desert of old red sandstone. The older sandstone was laid down much earlier than the limestone - around 345 million years ago as opposed to the Carboniferous period some 50 million years later.

However, in most places the younger rock has weathered away leaving the old red sandstone as the main skeleton of the National Park. Here, a thin layer of limestone remains and its summit looks white often giving the impression of being snow covered.

4. Shortly after leaving the summit trig point the ridge narrows and it is only a short distance to the west or left hand side of the plateau. Here you get a fantastic view of the Usk valley with the huge massif of the central Brecon Beacons as a backdrop. The distinctive flat tops of Pen y Fan and Corn Du slope down to the rich pastures below and the ridges of Bryn Teg and Cefn Cwm Lynch can be clearly seen. On a clear day it is possible to see the Carmarthen Fan and the Mynydd Du even further to the west, nearly 40 miles away. This is truly one of the most spectacular viewpoints in the National Park.

5. The route joins the Grwyne Fechan just below the summit of Waun Fach, the highest point of the Black Mountains. Here the infant river is no more than a trickle. It is, however, a far more scenic descent than the main path and always feels very isolated despite being only a few hundred metres away. As you follow its progress down the valley, it is fed by tributaries from both sides and becomes a quite powerful stream by the time it reaches the charming Tal-y-maes footbridge. Watch out along this stretch for dippers in the stream. These shy birds are slightly smaller than a blackbird with a white breast. They can be seen on rocks or even diving right under the water where they use their wings to swim whilst feeding on aquatic insects and larvae. This is also a good place to see herons wading in the pools looking for fish and also kestrels hovering above the banks. In autumn and winter the numerous thorn trees become home to redwings and fieldfares, members of the thrush family from Scandinavia who winter in Britain.

Walk Directions: (-) denotes point of interest.

1. Walk back to the bend in the road and climb over the stile on your right. Climb up through the field on the right hand side of the hedgerow to another stile.

2. Cross the narrow lane and another stile continuing upwards along the right hand side of a small wood. When you reach the drystone wall which divides the field from the open moors above, cross the stile and turn left, keeping the wall on your left as you follow the contours around the hill (1).

3. Continue to traverse the hill with the wall on your left for over a kilometre. The distinctive shape of Table Mountain will come into sight ahead to your right. Follow the path along the wall until you are directly below the hill itself and then take one of the many paths on your right aiming directly for its summit (2).

4. Having stopped to enjoy the views, take the clear path to the right off of the summit, this climbs at first quite gently and then more steeply towards the summit plateau of Pen Cerrig Calch. Once the plateau is reached then follow the path to the triangulation pillar (3).

5. Carry on in a generally northerly direction (4), dropping a few metres at first and then climbing again towards the summit of Pen Allt-mawr and another trig point.

6. Descend steeply from the summit of Pen Allt-mawr and then follow the path as it swings north west over a flat area for about a kilometre. Ignore the right fork at the end of this section and follow the main path due north along the escarpment edge for a kilometre, before veering north west and climbing Mynydd Llysiau.

7. After Mynydd Llysiau descend into the clear saddle to its north. This is a major junction of paths and a key resting place for walkers heading to Waun Fach. Here you need to drop down diagonally to your right. The path, which heads northeast is very clear.

8. After 150 metres the path turns very sharply right, instead of taking this, you should effectively carry straight on along a less distinct path which traverses the hillside. Follow this for approximately 500 metres and you will come to the infant Grwyne Fechan (5).

9. Cross the stream and turn right, following the bank as close to the river as you can. Occasionally it pays to cross the river to follow an easier path. For the next 3 kilometres just follow the river. After a

kilometre or so, you will find it easier to follow a clear track on the right hand bank.

10. When you arrive at Tal-y-maes bridge, this delightful section comes to an end and you must cross the bridge and follow the path up through the field and along a field boundary.

11. After a kilometre this path turns into a metalled road by Hermitage farm. This is actually the road you are parked on. From here it is about 3 kilometres straight on to the car.

Facilities

This is an isolated area and you will need to be self sufficient. There are public telephones to the north and south on the road on which you are parked. There is a pub and another public telephone at the village of Llanbedr.

Pen y Fan and Corn Du from the Storey Arms

The high mountains of the central Brecon Beacons by a circular route which encompasses the Tommy Jones Obelisk and some wide open moors.

OS maps:	1:50 000 Brecon Beacons 160
	1:25 000 Outdoor Leisure 12 Brecon Beacons National Park West and Central area.
Start:	Car park on the A470 opposite the Storey Arms Outdoor Education Centre. GR983203
Access:	By car, follow the A470 south from Brecon or north from Merthyr Tydfil. By bus, take the Silverline Service between Brecon and Merthyr Tydfil disembarking at Storey Arms.
Grade:	Easy - The easiest way to make a circular route of the highest peaks in the park. There is, however, still a fair amount of climbing involved and the summits are very exposed to the elements. An inexperienced walker should only attempt this route in good conditions.

Points of Interest:

1. Now an outdoor pursuits centre, the Storey Arms was once an Inn standing on the main green lane pass between the Brecon Beacons and Fforest Fawr. This lane would have been the main route for travellers and drovers who would have quenched their thirsts at the Inn. It takes its name from the family who ran it in those days. Later, when the A470 was built, it became a café before assuming its current guise.

2. The wild and open moorland around the summit of Y Gyrn gives the casual Brecon Beacons visitor a small taste of the isolation felt in much of the high ground of the National Park. It is hard to believe that

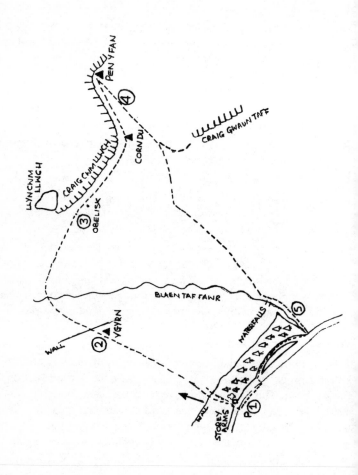

less than two kilometres away, on a good summer's day, hoards of people are making their way up to the high peaks on the well used path that will be your means of descent later in the day.

3. The Tommy Jones Obelisk stands proudly on the hillside above Llyn Cwm Llwch. It marks the spot where on the 2nd of September 1900, the body of five year old Tommy Jones was discovered after he'd been missing for almost a month.

On the 4th of August, Tommy and his father, a miner from the Rhondda valley, had caught the train to Brecon in order to visit Tommy's grandfather at his farm in Cwm Llwch. By the time they had reached Login which was then an army training camp, they had been travelling all day and young Tommy was getting tired. They rested and took refreshments at the camp and were met by Tommy's grandfather and his thirteen year old cousin, Willie. The two men stayed a while talking with the soldiers whilst the two boys set off alone for the farmhouse about ½ a mile away. As dusk started to fall, Tommy became unnerved in this strange new place and started to get upset. Willie had been told to inform the farm of the visitors arrival in the area and so he pressed on to the farmhouse whilst the small boy had decided to run back to his father and grandfather alone. Willie rejoined the men at Login about fifteen minutes later and discovered that Tommy hadn't arrived. Immediately the soldiers started a search but with no success. Soon the Police and other local people joined in but still found no trace of the boy.

Over the next few weeks the search continued. The *Daily Mail* offered a reward for information and people began to suspect that Tommy had been kidnapped or even murdered. Then in September, Mrs Hamer, a local woman, dreamt about the boy and, although she had never been there before, was able to lead her husband up to the ridge above Llyn Cwm Llwch where they were to discover Tommy's remains. The simple stone obelisk was erected after a public collection which included Mrs Hamer's *Daily Mail* reward of £20 and also the fees paid to the jury members at Tommy's inquest.

It is incredible to think that the boy had managed to walk over two miles to this spot, climbing over 400m including the steep, exposed stretch above the lake. He finally died of exposure, high on the hillside, serving as a tragic reminder to us all of the cruel and ruthless power of the Mountains. It is difficult to pass this spot without a pause for thought.

Incidentally, the obelisk was moved during the summer of 1997. The erosion had become so bad around its base that it was literally in danger of toppling over. It now stands closer to the main path and has even better views than before. The area surrounding the stone has been paved to avoid further erosion in the future.

4. Corn Du and Pen y Fan are not just the highest points in South Wales but also in the whole of southern Britain, the nearest higher ground being Cader Idris in North Wales some sixty miles away. The two summits are formed of the Upper Series of Old Red Sandstone known as Plateau Bed. This relatively hard stone hasn't weathered as much as the other types of rock and soil present and is therefore responsible for the table top structure of the peaks.

At 886m (2,906ft) Pen y Fan is just thirteen metres higher than its neighbour with both offering the extensive views you would expect from the highest point in the Park. As well as all the main ranges in the National Park it is possible, on a clear day, to see across the Bristol Channel to Exmoor and even the aforementioned Cader Idris sixty miles away. Sadly, being the highest place around also has its drawbacks and these summits can be a magnet to any cloud around, frequently hidden under a grey veil whilst the neighbouring peaks stay clear. This, however, only adds to the pleasure of experiencing a clear day. For maximum pleasure visit the summits early in the morning or just before sunset when the area becomes almost magical.

Excavations on these two peaks, as well as Cribyn to the east, have revealed Bronze Age burial cairns dated to 1800 BC. Back in those days the summits themselves may well have supported farming although it is difficult to imagine it in today's cooler, wetter climate.

5. A plaque by the side of the path here commemorates a very significant event in the history of the National Park. In 1965 the Eagle Star Insurance Company gave to the National Trust over 8,000 acres of land in the central Brecon Beacons. It was this gift, and the

continued management of the land by the National Trust, which ensures our future access to this magnificent countryside.

The Brecon Beacons are being "loved to death"

On this walk, as with many others along the high ridges of the National Park, it is difficult not to notice the ugly, scarring effect that the huge paths have on the mountain scenery. It is easy to imagine that these paths have always been there but this is, in fact, far from the truth. There has been more erosion in the National Park during the last 25 years than in the previous 100 million, since the withdrawing glaciers carved out the land into the shape it is today. The increase in the number of walkers has accelerated the problem but is not solely responsible. The erosion is caused by a number of factors, all of which interact to make the problem an escalating one.

Unlike many high mountain ranges the Brecon Beacons are not predominantly rocky underfoot, the under layers of rock are covered with a thin layer of soil which in turn supports vegetation. This vegetation then protects the soil from being washed away by running water, something which is in abundance, with over 200cm per year falling on the area. The vegetation, under constant threat from grazing and high altitude weather conditions, has only a tenuous hold in the poor quality soils and is therefore very fragile at the best of times.

Walking boots destroy the vegetation, leaving the resulting muddy ground to be quickly washed away. This then creates a channel that the water will begin to run down. Soon the path becomes waterlogged and the walker will tend to walk around the muddy, wet section, setting the whole cycle into motion again, this time with a wider path. In only a few years narrow sheep tracks have become as much as 30 metres wide and over a metre deep.

Since the mid 1970's when the problem first became recognised, various methods to control this erosion have been employed, some having more success than others. In general the later methods of stone pitching have been the most successful. This involves laying paths of available stone along the popular routes in a fashion not unlike the techniques used by the Romans. Generally two metres wide, the routes of the paths are chosen to make them the most desirable way to get the walker where he or she wants to go. Re-vegetation schemes are then carried out on each side of the path, helping it to blend in with the scenery. The size of the problem is astounding. In the Central Brecon Beacons alone over 7 kilometres of path have already been repaired whilst it is estimated that a further 45 kilometres will need doing if the current rates of erosion continue.

The work is carried out by teams from both the National Park Authority and the National Trust. With only a few full time officers much of the work is carried out by unpaid volunteers. The Ministry of Defence, who use the land regularly for training exercises, also assist by transporting huge bags of stone into position by helicopter.

So what can the walker do to help? In order to make minimum impact when in the hills, you should try to stay in single file on narrow sections, keep to the path when crossing boggy or muddy areas, follow any signposts or diversions that exist and try not to cut any corners. Where the path has been repaired, please keep to the stone section and avoid walking along the grass next to it, even if it feels softer on tired feet at the end of a long, hard day.

Walk Directions: (-) denotes point of interest.

1. From the car park, cross the A470 and go through the gate on the left hand side of the Storey Arms (1). Follow the main path for about 20 metres then fork left onto a grassy, less obvious path and carry on for another 100 metres before reaching a wall.

2. Carry straight on through the wall, climbing gently towards the summit of Y Gyrn ahead and to your left.

3. On the top of Y Gyrn you will come to a broken down wall with a fence backing it up. Cross the fence at the stile then bear slightly left for about 10 metres before turning right and heading down the hill into the shallow valley below (2).

4. The path should be fairly easy to follow as it crosses the valley and climbs up the other side, always trending to the right. Approximately 1

kilometre further on, you will see the huge valley of Cwm Llwch on your left hand side with Llyn Cwm Llwch directly below you.

5. The path will lead you directly to Craig Cwm Llwch and the Obelisk (3). From here, carry on up the hill with the cliffs to your left. This will lead you to the summit of Corn Du now visible on the horizon above you.

6. From the summit of Corn Du, carry on eastwards towards Pen y Fan dropping slightly before a gentle climb to the summit cairn (4).

7. Retrace your steps off of Pen y Fan, forking left just before it levels off. Follow this clear path under the summit of Corn Du, carrying straight on at any junctions until you start to descend.

8. You can now follow this path as it descends the side of the valley to join up with the Blaen Taf Fawr (5). Carry on along the side of the river for a few hundred metres before crossing it on stepping stones and going through a gate into the car park.

9. Turn right and walk through the car park eventually emerging back onto the A470. Turn right and carry on a few hundred metres to the Storey Arms.

Facilities

There is free car parking opposite the Storey Arms or alternatively, in the lay-by to the south east of this. The nearest public telephone is next to the Storey Arms and there are public toilets in the lay-by.

There are often snack vans in the lay-by but there are no pubs or shops nearby.

The Mountain Centre at Libanus is approximately 7 kilometres north of the start of this walk and the Forest Centre at Garwnant a similar distance to the south.

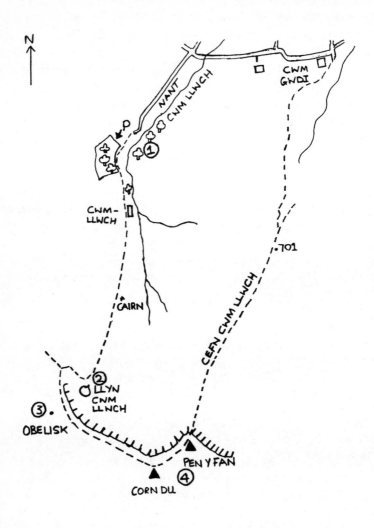

N

NANT
CWM LLWCH
CWM GWDI
P
① ① ① ①
① ①
CWM-LLWCH
· 701
CEFN CWM LLWCH
✝ CAIRN
②
LLYN CWM LLWCH
③ ·
OBELISK
CORN DU
④
PEN Y FAN

Twin Peaks - Pen y Fan and Corn Du from Cwm Llwch.

A varied mountain walk along clear paths including the highest summits in the National Park and the touching Tommy Jones Obelisk.

OS maps:	1:50 000 Brecon Beacons 160 1:25 000 Outdoor Leisure 12 Brecon Beacons National Park West and Central area.
Start:	Car park at Cwm Llwch. GR006244
Access:	This walk is only really accessible by car. It is best reached by following a minor road southwest from Brecon or by following minor roads west from Llanfrynach.
Grade:	Moderate - A mixture of high mountain and riverside walking on good paths - one long but gentle climb with a short steep section midway.

Points of Interest:

1. The car parking area at Nant Cwm Llwch is in a delightful riverside position with open areas of grass, ideal for a picnic or just a restful afternoon in the countryside. The trees surrounding the river and the stony path to Login are full of wildlife, with squirrels darting about collecting whatever food they can find and a wide variety of bird life.

By the river look out for pied and grey wagtails, easily identifiable by their long tails which usually wag up and down. The pied wagtail, as its name suggests is mainly black and white whilst its grey cousin has a slate grey back and a sulphur yellow breast. Like many of the streams in the National Park you may also see dippers here, particularly on a quieter day.

In and around the trees pied flycatchers can be seen. Although naturally quite shy, they dart back and forth from their perches catching insects. About the size of a sparrow they are easily recognisable by the males strong black and white plumage. Also keep your eyes peeled for treecreepers. This small, mouse like little bird ghosts up and down tree trunks searching the cracks in the bark for insects and larvae. It can be difficult to spot as it is a dull, mottled brown in colour but can easily be heard uttering a high "treep" sound. With similar habits but much more colourful is the nuthatch. It has a grey/blue back and a buff and red underside with a black streak over the eye. It is really quite a treat to watch as it creeps up and down the tree trunks in search of food. Also found in this delightful little bird watching area are many species of tits including blue tits, great tits and long tailed tits.

2. Whilst the other main mountain ranges in the British Isles have seemingly as many lakes as they do mountains, the Brecon Beacons are an exception. Llyn Cwm Llwch is one of only a handful of glacial formed lakes in the National Park. The steep sides of Corn Du and Pen y Fan at the head of Cwm Llwch were formed when the existing valley was gradually enlarged by direct glacial action. The debris carried by the glacier would have been deposited near the outflow creating a dam of earth and boulders known as moraine. This moraine would then have held back the melt water forming the small lake or Llyn in Welsh. This is a great place to stop and get your breath back before the final push to the top.

3. The Tommy Jones Obelisk stands proudly on the hillside above the Llyn. It marks the spot where on 2nd of September 1900, five year old Tommy's body was discovered after he'd been missing for almost a month. (See Walk 5)

Walk Directions: (-) denotes point of interest.

1. Starting in the car park (1), walk along the track with the river to

your left. You will cross a footbridge before coming to a building.

2. Follow the signs to the right of the building and over two stiles in quick succession. You now rejoin the track and continue on up hill alongside small trees until you reach the stile on the boundary of the National Trust land and the open hillside.

3. Stay on the main path past a large broken down cairn heading all the time towards the far right hand side of the head of the valley. When you reach Llyn Cwm Llwch (2) the path turns quite sharply to the right and climbs steeply up the hillside to the ridge above.

4. When you join the ridge turn to your left and follow the path past the obelisk (3) towards the summit of Corn Du which will now be clearly visible above you. Carry on to the summit where you will climb, steeply, the final few metres to the summit cairn.

5. From the summit of Corn Du you will see to the east your final objective, the summit of Pen y Fan. Follow the path in the direction of Pen y Fan, at first dropping a few metres before a final brief climb takes you to the summit of the highest ground in southern Britain (4) (see Walk 5). Take care to follow any instructions about diverted footpaths on this section as the area suffers from dreadful erosion and a considerable amount of effort is being put into regenerating vegetation on the hilltop. See the separate feature in this book about footpath erosion and maintenance (Walk 5).

6. After admiring the views and regaining your breath it is time to start your descent. Head due north to the edge from the summit cairn and you will notice a very steep path down the sharp ridge separating the two Cwms. Take this path, taking considerable care on the steep and sometimes loose ground.

7. When the ground eventually flattens out you can enjoy the ridge of Cefn Cwm Llwch for the next kilometre or so without having to give much thought to route finding. You will eventually climb slightly and arrive at the spot height marked 701m on the map. Just after this you will see paths off to the right and left.

8. Stay on the main, most clearly defined path heading almost due north and descending the centre of the shoulder down from the ridge.

This is shown as a small, dotted line on the map.

9. After a short distance a new valley opens out in front of you. Continue on down the main track which actually traverses the left (west) side of the valley. This track widens into a terrace as it descends.

10. Carry on along this path until it reaches almost level ground. Here you cross a stile and carry on to the car park directly in front of you.

11. There is now a little road walking to return to the start. Carry on through the car park and down the hill past some old Ministry of Defence buildings. After 200 metres, take a left turn.

12. Follow this lane for approximately one kilometre, passing a turning on the right and a farm lane on the left. You will then drop down a short hill and across a bridge. Immediately after the bridge you come to a crossroads, turn left and follow this lane for approximately half a kilometre to the car park at the start of the walk.

Facilities

Free car parking in the car park at Nant Cwm Llwch which makes a great picnic area and children's playground.

The nearest public telephones, pubs and shops are either Brecon or Llanfrynach.

The National Park Visitors Centre or Mountain Centre is only a few kilometres from the start of this walk at Libanus. See walk 10, The Mountain Centre, for more details.

Walk 7   *7½ miles/12 kilometres*
                                              4-5 hours

Pen y Fan and Corn Du
from the Neuadd Reservoirs

The high mountains of the central Brecon Beacons from the south, taking in some spectacular ridges and an ancient road.

OS maps: 1:50 000 Brecon Beacons 160
              1:25 000 Outdoor Leisure 12 Brecon Beacons National
              Park West and Central area.

Start: Junction of the Taff Trail with the minor road leading to
              the Neuadd Reservoirs.GR035174

Access: By car, either follow the minor road from Talybont on
              Usk past the Talybont Reservoir and turning sharp right
              at the t-junction with the road north from Pontsticill or
              follow the road north from Pontsticill past the Pontsticill
              Reservoir. There are many roadside parking places both
              to the north and the south of the start.

Grade: Moderate - a long gentle ascent to start with, followed
              by some fairly strenuous climbs to the summits. The
              final descent to the reservoirs is fairly steep. As this is a
              high level route it can be very exposed to the elements.
              It is possible to avoid the ascent of any of the three
              peaks in this walk by clear paths on their southern slopes
              making the route considerably easier.

Points of Interest:

1. Once you begin to gain height you will see, on your left, the two
Neuadd Reservoirs. The lower reservoir, nearest to the start of the
walk, was constructed in 1884 to supply the water to the then booming
town of Merthyr Tydfil. As the iron, steel and coal production in the
area continued to expand, demand outstripped supply and a second

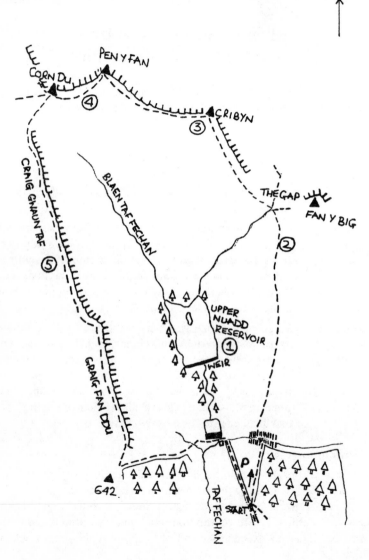

N

PEN Y FAN

CORN DU

④

③

CRIBYN

THE GAP

FAN Y BIG

②

CRAIG GWAUN TAF

BLAEN TAF FECHAN

⑤

UPPER
NUADD
RESERVOIR

①

WEIR

GRAIG FAN DDU

642.

P

TAF FECHAN

START

60

dam was constructed higher up the valley. The reservoirs, now surrounded by woodland including many beautiful scots pines, make a great spot for a picnic.

2. The track you are following up the valley is often referred to as the "gap road" as it leads to Bwlch ar y Fan, the saddle between Fan y Big and Cribyn, which is commonly known as "the gap". It is often thought of as a Roman Road and is certainly ancient in origin. It may well have been used by the heavy Roman presence in the area to get through the high peaks of the central Brecon Beacons to link forts in the north such as Y Gaer with others further south near Merthyr Tydfil. There is, however, no firm evidence that this is the case. It is at "the gap" that you enter land now owned by the National Trust, having been given to them and, therefore, the people of our land, by the Eagle Star Insurance Company in 1965.

3. Once at the summit of Cribyn it is easy to see the architecture of this magnificent mountain range in its full glory. The steep slopes to the north are known as scarp slopes, and were sculpted by glacial action on the land. The easier angled slopes to the south are known as the dip slopes. This formation is typical of all glacial formed mountain ranges. From this summit, itself 795 metres, there are great views of Pen y Fan which is your next objective. You will also clearly see a huge scar on the landscape which is the path from Cribyn to Pen y Fan. (See the feature on path erosion elsewhere in this book.) (Walk 5)

4. See Pen y Fan. (Direction no. 4; Walk 5)

5. The path along Craig Gwaun Taf, Rhiw yr Ysgyfarnog and Graig Fan Ddu offers over three kilometres of the highest quality ridge walking, never dropping below two thousand feet. The steep scarp slopes drop hundreds of feet, almost vertically, to your left whilst the magnificent valley of Cwm Crew opens out to your right. It really is a very airy view point. To your right you will also see the huge lumpy summit of Fan Fawr at the eastern edge of the Fforest Fawr range, this itself is well worth exploring on another day.

All along the crag edge keep your eyes open for the arial displays of the ravens that frequent this habitat. These huge members of the crow family are masters of flight and perform endless tricks, climbing

61

and swooping on invisible air currents. Often heard before they are seen, their call is a flat "gronk" sound. Other bird species seen along this elevated walkway include meadow pipits, skylarks and wheatears. During the summer months swifts, swallows and house martins will also be in abundance, twisting and turning in flight as they catch insects on the wing.

Walk Directions: (-) denotes point of interest.

1. From your car, walk along the road until you reach the junction of two paths with the road itself. From here take the left of the two paths, heading north with the woods on your right.

2. From here, your navigation worries are over for a while as you follow this path beyond the woods, across a steep sided gorge and out into open mountain country(1) (2). For the next 2 kilometres continue, climbing steadily, along the path.

3. When you do arrive at "the gap" the saddle between Fan y Big to your right and Cribyn to your left, the path to your left, up the steep grassy slope of Cribyn becomes obvious. Take this path and follow it to the summit (3).

4. From the summit cairn, turn left and descend the clear path towards Pen y Fan. The ground will eventually flatten off before continuing on, this time upwards, to the summit of Pen y Fan (4).

5. Again from the summit cairn, turn left and descend slightly before a short steep climb takes you to the obvious summit of Corn Du. From here track left again and after 100 metres you will be in Bwlch Duwynt, the saddle between Corn Du and Craig Gwaun Taf.

6. Continue heading south with the steep escarpment on your left and the main path back down to Storey Arms on your right. Once above the crags which have now appeared to your left, you can again forget navigation for a while as the ridge extends for well over 2 kilometres (5).

7. Continue along the ridge until you can see a forested area below on

the hillside to your left and a trig point at 642 metres in front of you. Above the corner of the wood take the steep path on your left which descends towards the lower reservoir with the woods on your right.

8. Once you reach the reservoir, go through the gate, carry on along the path, across the reservoir outlet and up a short hill to a derelict building on your left. At the end of the building, there is a small gate which leads onto the road. Follow the road back to your car.

Facilities

This is a fairly isolated spot and it is advisable to be self sufficient.
There are public telephones, toilets, shops and pubs in the village of Pontsticill.

N

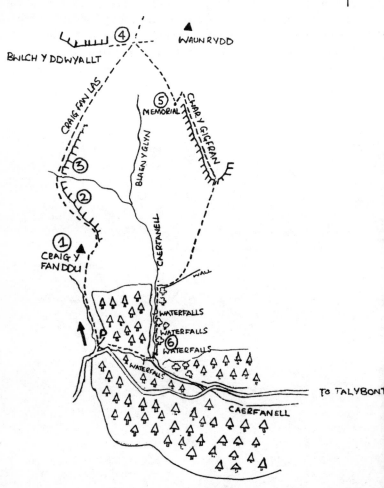

BWLCH Y DDWYALLT

④

WAUN RYDD

CRAIG FAN LAS

⑤
MEMORIAL

CHWAR Y GIGFRAN

③

②

BLAEN Y GLYN

CAERFANELL

①
CRAIG Y
FAN DDU

WALL

WATERFALLS

WATERFALLS

⑥ WATERFALLS

WATERFALL

TO TALYBONT

CAERFANELL

Craig y Fan Ddu - Waun Rydd War Memorial - Blaen y Glyn Waterfall

OS maps: 1:50 000 Brecon Beacons 160:
                1:25 000 Outdoor Leisure 12 Brecon Beacons National Park West and Central area.

Start: Forest Walk car park on the Talybont on Usk to Pontstiscill Rd. GR056175.

Access: This walk is only really accessible by car. It is best reached by turning left off the B4558 in Talybont on Usk and following the minor road through the village of Aber alongside the Talybont reservoir.

Grade: Moderate - A mixture of high open moorland and riverside walking - mainly on good paths - one fairly steep climb at the start, two small steep climbs later on.

Points of Interest:

1. The biggest rewards for walking in the hills are the views and this route proves no exception. From the top of Craig y Fan Ddu the views reach in all directions. To the north west you can see the table top summit of Pen y Fan which at 886m is the highest point in the National Park and, in fact, South Wales. It sits majestically next to its twin peak Corn Du *(The Black Horn)*. These two hills themselves are the subjects of other routes in this book.

To the South you will see the summit and ridge of Pant y Creigiau, unusual for its limestone formation in this otherwise mainly sandstone area. Below this the Talybont Forest can be seen running the whole length of the Talybont Reservoir. Offering a mixture of broad-leaved native trees as well as larch and spruce it shows off a much more attractive autumn vista than most of the Welsh pine forests.

To the East you have the vast amphitheatre of Cerrig Edmwnt

crowned by the crags of Cwar y Gigfran. You will get a much closer look at these later in the walk. Beyond these the peaty plateaus of Waun Rydd is an excellent example of the less frequented yet equally stunning upland landscape of the National Park.

2. The spectacular escarpment on your right drops almost vertically downwards for over 50m in places. These sandstone ridges run almost the full width of the park and are responsible for its form and shape. Often over-hanging the grassy slopes below by over a metre, they offer spectacular photo opportunities for the sure footed walker. This is a glacial landscape shaped by huge ice rivers that have softened the valleys into this characteristic u-shape.

3. The area is home to many species of birds. The crag itself is an ideal place to see ravens, the largest member of the crow family and real aerial acrobats. Great pleasure can be had from watching their aerobatics displays as they soar on rising air currents before diving at high speed, often spinning in flight. Kestrels and buzzards can also be seen fairly regularly, the kestrel hovering almost motionless seeking its quarry with incredible eyesight, whilst the buzzard circles effortlessly above on the updraughts. Closer to the ground you will see skylarks and meadow pipits. The former is always a delight in spring as it leads you away from its nest, usually hidden in the grass somewhere close by. If you don't see one, you will almost certainly hear one as it hovers above you performing a shrill, seemingly endless chorus. Wheatear are also commonplace up here. A little larger than a sparrow, the male is an attractive grey with a strong black stripe over the eye and an orangey yellow breast. Both sexes are easily recognised by a white rump as they fly away, usually short distances to the next safe rock.

4. At this point the views are to the North. Here you will see the Cathedral and market town of Brecon. Named after the 5th century Welsh prince Brychan, (in Welsh, *Brycheiniog*), Brecon has maintained much of its medieval feel with over 500 protected buildings.

The town now has a population of over 7,500 that swells considerably with its tourist trade in the summer. As well as the

National Park itself, the fine Cathedral attracts many visitors as does the canal, where it is possible to hire or stay on a narrowboat.

Much closer to you are the cwms of Oergwm and Cwareli. The mountain streams that wind their way down the valley eventually join forces before flowing into the River Usk at Llanfrynach.

To your left you will see clear views of Pen y Fan, Corn Du, Cribyn and even closer Fan y Big.

5. On July 6th 1942, during a night training flight, Wellington Bomber R 1465 came down in bad weather killing all five Canadian crew members on board. The twisted wreckage of their plane lies where it fell and the spot is marked by a memorial cairn, usually draped in poppy wreaths. The Brecon Beacons were frequently used during World War II as a training and practice ground and inevitably there were other crashes in the area. This scene, however, is one of total serenity and few could stop here without being moved. It would be easy to wonder whether the young men who fell here had the chance to savour the beautiful mountains of their own country during their all too short lives.

6. The Blaen y Glyn waterfall is the largest of the many waterfalls along the Caerfanell river as it plummets down from the hills above. Tumbling 15m to crash on huge slabs of rock, it is a truly spectacular sight. In winter it can become frozen solid, forming huge icicles, whilst in summer it is not unusual to see sunbathers using it as a cold shower in this popular picnic area.

On quiet days look out for dippers in the stream, these shy birds are slightly smaller than a blackbird with a white breast. They can be seen on rocks or even diving right under the water, where they use their wings to swim whilst feeding on aquatic insects and larvae.

As you climb up through the wood after crossing the footbridge there are many other waterfalls on both sides, some supporting fine hanging gardens of ferns and rowan trees as well as many mosses and lichens.

Walk Directions: (-) denotes point of interest.

1. Starting in the car park walk back towards the road until you cross the cattle grid. Take the clear path on your right, leading up the hill alongside the stream. When the path leaves the stream and heads slightly right it begins to steepen. Follow this to the top (1).

2. After catching your breath, follow the path as it trends around to the right and joins the ridge above the East facing escarpment of Craig y Fan Ddu (2) (3). Your route finding is over for a while as you follow the ridge for nearly 2 kilometres. When the once deep valley on your right flattens out and you meet a path crossing yours at right angles the views now will be directly ahead of you to the North (4).

3. You will notice that the path to the right splits into two here with one heading up towards the hills and one turning slightly downhill and slightly back on yourself. Take this second path and follow it in the direction of the cliffs you can see in front of you (Cwar y Gigfran). Just over half a kilometre along this path, nestled underneath the crag you will see the Canadian War Memorial (5).

4. Directly above the memorial you will see a rocky gully. On its left can be seen a steep, indistinct grassy path leading to the top of the crag. Take this path until it meets a major path coming in from the left. Turn right and walk along the ridge following the path to a large cairn. From the cairn follow the path that continues straight on and drops downhill steeply in a grassy groove. This path then meets a wall where you turn right and follow it down to the Caerfanell stream and a stile.

5. Upon reaching the stream turn left over the stile and follow the path past a succession of waterfalls (6). At the Blaen y Glyn Waterfall you will see a footbridge over the stream. Turn right over the footbridge then, after crossing the stile, turn left into the woodlands.

6. A few metres along this path take a right turn into the woods, clearly marked by a green pole with a blue top. This path is now clearly marked as it climbs up through the woods between two streams. You may however wish to take a small detour to the left or right to view other waterfalls. Follow the path up hill steeply through the trees

where it will lead you back to the car-park you started from.

Facilities

Free car-parking in the National Trust car parks both at the start of the walk and also just down the road at the Pont Blaen y Glyn.

Public telephones can be found at Aber, Pontsticill and Talybont on Usk.

There is often an ice-cream vendor at the dam of the Talybont reservoir also shops and pubs can be found in Talybont on Usk.

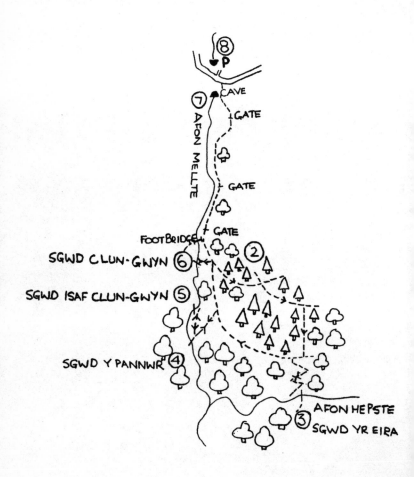

N

⑧ P

CAVE

⑦ GATE

AFON MELLTE

GATE

GATE

FOOTBRIDGE

SGWD CLUN-GWYN ⑥ ②

SGWD ISAF CLUN-GWYN ⑤

SGWD Y PANNWR ④

AFON HEPSTE

③ SGWD YR EIRA

The Waterfalls Walk

A short and fairly gentle walk through mixed woodland, steep sided gorges and the most spectacular waterfalls in the National Park.

OS maps:	1:50 000 Brecon Beacons 160 1:25 000 Outdoor Leisure 12 Brecon Beacons National Park West and Central area.
Start:	Car park near Porth yr Ogof approximately one kilometre south of Ystradfellte. GR928123. There is a parking fee of £2.00.
Access:	This walk is only really accessible by car. It is best reached by following the minor road north west from the A4059 to Ystradfellte or from the west by following the minor road north from Pontneddfechan.
Grade:	Easy - The walk follows well marked paths and the short steep sections have wooden steps and handrails. Take care as the rocks around the waterfalls can be extremely slippery. It is advisable to keep children under close supervision, particularly near the rivers and waterfalls.

Points of Interest:

1. Around Ystradfellte, a dramatic geological change takes place. As the rivers Mellte, Hepste and Nedd flow down from the hills of Fforest Fawr they leave behind the harder old red sandstone that makes up most of the mountains in the National Park and rush headlong into younger, softer, soluble limestone. Here they carve out deep gorges and form deep underground caverns. Having carved these gorges, the rivers now drop steeply and begin to flow much faster. It is here that they meet a layer of harder millstone grit. Where faulting has occurred, the river bed has become a mixture of hard grit and soft shale. Over

71

the passage of thousands of years, the river has worn down the softer shale and now plummets over sharply defined shelves of the harder rock, forming the waterfalls we see today.

2. The mixed woodlands along the route are as much a feature of this walk as the waterfalls. Keep your eyes open for the abundance of wildlife it supports. Grey squirrels will dart across the path in front of you, scrambling for safety up a nearby tree. In winter when times are harder they tend to be less wary and it is possible to watch them scurrying around in the undergrowth seeking food. Undoubtedly, it is their climbing skills that are most interesting, seemingly able to jump great distances, landing on vertical tree trunks and then climbing up or down with equal ease.

Amongst the birdlife in the forest you will see nuthatches, treecreepers, many small tits, chaffinches, robins and wrens. In the rivers themselves wagtails and dippers hop from rock to rock. As always when you get so many small birds together, look out for sparrowhawks gliding low over the forest looking for unsuspecting prey.

Should you be lucky enough to visit this area in the Autumn, the colours of the trees make a beautiful backdrop for the magnificent falls and rapids.

3. Sgwd yr Eira (or the *Falls of Snow*) is the most famous of the waterfalls on this route. Although it isn't the highest it is certainly the most memorable. A path actually runs behind the waterfall, allowing the walker a spectacular view of the torrent of water plummeting down nearly eight metres. The noise is deafening and it is well worth wearing waterproofs if the river is in spate as the falls create their own wind which, in turn, blows the spray in all directions. It is said that farmers would have used this path to herd their livestock over the river. That certainly would have been a spectacle! Unlike many well publicised places, Sgwd yr Eira doesn't disappoint. It is certainly one of the jewels of the National Park.

4. The next main waterfall you will see is Sgwd y Pannwr. This translates to the *Fuller's Falls* although the reason for its name isn't obvious. It wouldn't have made sense for a Fuller to walk this far, past

other waterfalls, just to full his cloth at this one. Whatever the reason for the name, it is certainly a fine waterfall and the flat area above it makes a great place to view its power and grace.

5. Next along is Sgwd Isaf Clun-gwyn (or the *Lower Falls of the White Meadow*). It is possible with great care to scramble down to the rocky ledge at water level. From here you will see that, in fact, the fall is in two levels, dropping nearly 30 metres in total. What makes it even more scenic is the fact that the faults that created it don't run at right angles to the river so the falls themselves seem to come at you from all angles.

6. The final falls on the walk, Sgwd Clun-gwyn (or the *White Meadow Falls)*, really do emphasise the way the falls were formed. From above, the river seems to flow quite peacefully along the flat area of harder rock before suddenly reaching the falls. Here the softer shale has worn away creating a drop of ten metres in total over two steps. The step quite clearly shows the way the rock is layered. At the foot of the falls there are some strange rock formations, again created by the blend of soft and hard rock. It is possible, though not necessarily advisable, to walk across the falls at the top in dryer weather, where the water is concentrated on the eastern bank.

7. At the resurgence cave, just downstream from the road, it is possible to follow a cavers path over the top of the cave and view some swallow holes or pot holes. These are formed where the surface water sets to work on weaknesses in the soluble limestone cave roof eventually forming funnel shaped holes which join into the cave below. These are fenced off to the public but great care should be exercised when near their edges.

8. Porth yr Ogof (literally the *Door of the Cave*) is the largest cave entrance in Wales. It is one of many entrances to a complex cave system, some of which is still unexplored. It is possible to walk a little way inside the cave in dryer weather and see the Pool of the White Horse, named after the resemblance to a horse's head of some of the calcite streaks on its back wall. Legend has it that a princess once rode her white steed into the cave trying to outsmart the murderous intentions of her pursuers. The horse fell and both were drowned - the

horses head on the wall a sad tribute to them both. Heed the notices in the area and take great care near the caves and waterfalls as the river runs fast and could easily catch out the unwary.

Walk Directions: (-) denotes point of interest.

1. Walk out of the car park, straight across the road and follow the footpath as signposted. After a few metres you will come to a large stile which is signposted "for cavers only". Follow the path leftwards around this and through a kissing gate with the pasture on your left.

2. The route here is easy to follow as you carry on along the path through scrubland and onto the grassy banks of the river Mellte. Continue along the river bank with the river on your right and through two more gates until it swings to the left and you walk past a footbridge.

3. Carrying along, on the same side of the river, you must scramble up a rocky section of the path into the woods (2). Keep to the left now until, at the top of the hill, the path forks in front of you at the edge of a coniferous wood. Take the left hand path around the right hand side of the wood until you come to a crossroads.

4. Take the right hand turning signposted to Sgwd yr Eira. Follow this path for a few hundred metres until another signpost directs you right again and down a steep hill. At the bottom of this section turn right again and then left down the steep steps to Sgwd yr Eira (3). To walk behind the falls, walk along the river bank ascending gently onto the stone pavement which then runs to the other bank.

5. Retrace your route back up the steps to the path above and turn left following it up the hill to the boundary of a wood. Here a signpost directs you to Sgwd y Pannwr and Sgwd Isaf Clun-gwyn. Follow the path to Sgwd y Pannwr (4).

6. From the falls carry on upstream along the side of the river for 400m to Sgwd Isaf Clun-gwyn (5). To see the falls better you will need to scramble down a tricky small path. From here, again retrace your steps back along the river to Sgwd y Pannwr and then back up the hill to the main path where you turn left towards the last waterfall of

the walk.

7. You will now come to the junction of the paths that you turned away from the river at earlier. Turn left here and follow the path to the Sgwd Clun-gwyn viewing area (6). Retrace your steps back to the junction of paths and turn left again.

8. From now on you are reversing the path you took along the river on the way out. Go past the footbridge and through the gates until you reach the grassy area on the bank of the river. In front of you now is the resurgence cave.

9. After viewing the resurgence cave, follow the original path back towards the car park. To see the swallow holes (7) cross the stile marked for cavers only.

10. Cross the road and back into the car park where you can follow a path down some steps on its left hand side to view Porth yr Ogof (8).

Facilities

There is an admission charge to the car park where public toilets and a telephone are available. There is also a small picnic area.

There is a pub and shops in Ystradfellte itself.

There are other woodland walks and a picnic area one kilometre away at Gwaun Hepste.

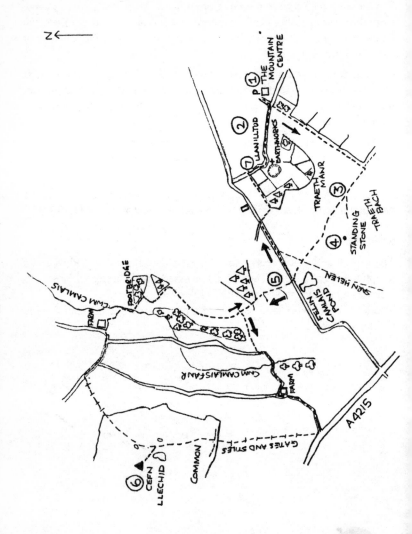

N ←

① THE MOUNTAIN CENTRE
P
② LLANILLTUD
EARTHWORKS
⑦
TRAETH MAWR
③
④ STANDING STONE
TRAETH BACH
SARN HELEN
FELINS CAMLAIS POND
⑤
CWM CAMLAIS
FOOTBRIDGE
FARM
CWM CAMLAIS FAWR
FARM
A 4215
GATES AND STILES
COMMON
⑥ CEFN LLECHID

The Mountain Centre - Mynydd Illtud Common - Cefn Llechid

A half day country ramble suitable for all the family with extensive views over the high mountains of the National Park. Can be combined with a visit to the Mountain Centre.

OS maps:	1:50 000 Brecon Beacons 160
	1:25 000 Outdoor Leisure 12 Brecon Beacons National Park West and Central area.
Start:	The Mountain Centre at Libanus. GR976263
Access:	By car, from the A470 at Libanus, follow the signs to the Mountain Centre. By bus, take the Silverline service between Brecon and Merthyr Tydfil, disembarking at Libanus. The Mountain Centre is approximately 2 kilometres from here. Throughout the year there are events and activities laid on at the Mountain Centre. It may be possible to get a bus directly to the Mountain Centre on these occasions, check for details.
Grade:	Easy - Although a longish walk, the going is generally fairly easy on well marked paths. The ascents are reasonably easy, though there is a fairly steep descent from Cefn Llechid.

Points of Interest:

1. The route starts at the Mountain Centre on Mynydd Illtud Common. This is the main visitor centre for the National Park and contains an absolute wealth of information about the surrounding area. As well as tea rooms and tidy grounds with wonderful views over the hills of the central Brecon Beacons, the centre has year round displays, talks, film

shows, a shop and even organises local walks. It is well worth a visit.

2. Mynydd Illtud Common, now home to a nature reserve and Cefn Llechid (to be visited later on this walk), were originally common land as designated by the manorial system of the Normans. Commoners in the area had certain rights of access to the land which was usually unsuitable for crops. These included grazing, fishing, peat digging and the removal of stone, minerals and soil. The Lord retained all of the hunting and shooting rights. With developments in agricultural methods it became easier to cultivate crops on this type of land leading to the Enclosures Act being passed allowing the Lords to "buy" these rights back from the commoners. All common land is now registered as such and is still essential to some communities for grazing. The two areas of common land in this walk are actually owned by the National Park Authority.

3. The boggy area at the south western end of the common is now a Site of Special Scientific Interest or SSSI. This includes Traeth Mawr and Traeth Bach, the Great Mire and the Little Mire which are important habitats for many bog plants as well as wildfowl and waders. At the very edge of the common is the Felin Camlais pond. Here it is possible to see herons, mallard ducks, teal, snipe, curlews and other waders, as well as swallows and swifts catching insects on the wing. Other birds often seen include raptors such as buzzards, sparrowhawks, the dainty little hobby and, if you are particularly lucky, even the red kite. (See page 85)

4. Near Felin Camlais pond is a small standing stone (GR963255) which can be reached by backtracking along the fenced boundary of the common for some 500 metres. Although it doesn't look much in itself, the stone lines up directly with another stone at the north eastern end of the common and also with the ancient earthworks at Llanilltud. Incredibly, all three line up with the position of the sunrise at the summer solstice and, from Llanilltud, the sunrise at the winter solstice can be seen between the twin summits of Pen y Fan and Corn Du. This takes place at right angles to the alignment of the stones. The stones themselves are almost certainly Bronze Age in origin and as the summits of the mountains were the sites of Bronze Age burial cairns, it

is easy to deduce that these people were very aware of the movements of the sun and placed great importance upon them.

The path near the pond also crosses another landmark of historical importance, the Sarn Helen Roman road. This road, which linked forts at Neath with Y Gaer, near Brecon, is more spectacular in other areas of the National Park, in particular north of Ystradfellte. It forms part of a long distance road linking North and South Wales.

5. Only minutes after leaving a Roman road you will find yourself walking another historic track, this time an original drovers road. In use until the end of the last century, drove roads were used by the drovers, a kind of cowhand, to move cattle, sheep, pigs and even geese and turkeys hundreds of miles to market. The main routes of the time would have meant incurring large tolls whilst the quiet routes, often crossing open countryside, were much cheaper allowing the animals to graze freely whilst traveling and, consequently, arriving in better condition for sale.

6. Cefn Llechid, at only 400 metres, seems like a small foothill in the distinguished company of the surrounding mountains. It does, however, afford magnificent views over the highest mountains of the National Park and is high enough that it would be considered an important summit in many of Southern England's hilly areas such as the Quantock Hills and the Mendips. To the west you will see the vast sweep of the Carmarthen Fan in the Mynydd Du or Black Mountain and, to the east, the valleys of the Black Mountains. This truly is one of the great view points of the National Park.

7. Before returning to the Mountain Centre you will pass the previously mentioned site of Llanilltud, once a Bronze Age settlement and more recently the site of St Illtud's church. The church, however, was derelict for many years before being demolished in 1995. The graveyard itself tells stories of hard times and short life expectancies. It is quite fascinating to think that the church was built on what was probably a site used for Pagan worship thousands of years earlier. To see the winter solstice from this unique position, guided walks are often organised from the Mountain Centre.

Walk Directions: (-) denotes point of interest.

1. Walk out of the car park, turn left back to the road which you then cross and carry on across the common with the wall on your left for approximately 1 kilometre (2).

2. You will pass 2 footpath signs on your left. At the second, fork right across the common (3). After a few hundred metres fork right and carry on along the clear path to the road with the pond on your left. Backtrack along the common boundary for 500 metres to see the standing stone (4).

3. Cross the road at the pond and directly opposite you is a walled lane which you now proceed along (5). Go through two gates, then shortly before a third take a track to your left which descends into the valley.

4. At the bottom of the hill you meet a metalled road. Turn left, go over the bridge at the bottom before ascending again past a farmhouse on your left. After the farm there is a small junction. Keep to the left, going behind the farmhouse and continuing for approximately 600 metres to the main A4215.

5. Here, take a path to your right, through a gate and carry on along this bridleway for over 1 kilometre, crossing numerous stiles and gates all the way. At the top of the hill a final gate gives you access to the common land beyond.

6. Once on the common carry on straight ahead, past a pond on your left. At the end of the pond a left fork will take you to the trig point on the summit (6). From here retrace your steps back to the pond, turning left on to the path you started on.

7. From here, carry on across the common until you meet a gate which signifies the end of the common land. Cross the gate, keep straight ahead and descend in a sunken lane to the road below.

8. Turn right onto the road and follow it past two turnings on your right until you come to a farm at the bottom of the hill. Turn right into the farmyard which you then cross to a gate in the far corner.

9. Go through the gate and follow the track to the right as it drops into the valley. Cross the river Nant Camlais Fach by the wooden

footbridge and head uphill through the woods with the wall on your right and the stream to your left.

10. Shortly you will emerge from the woodland into an open field. Turn right here following the sunken path along the bottom of the field before swinging left up hill to a gate.

11. The path crosses the fence on its right and follows another fence up hill, here it is clearly lined with birch trees. Carry on along the path, through a number of gates and stiles, until you come to the junction where earlier in the walk you had turned left. Carry straight on past this lane, through two more gates and back onto the common.

12. Turn left onto the road and carry on for 700 metres until another road joins from the left. At this point you can turn right off of the road and onto the common. Head for the edge of a wood, turning left along the fence as you reach it.

13. Follow the fence until you come out onto a road. Turn right here and follow it to Llanilltud (7). You can enter the graveyard on the right if you wish. Carry on along this road until it once again, crosses the common, before turning left at the next junction to return to the Mountain Centre.

Facilities

There are public toilets, a public telephone and tea rooms at the Mountain Centre. The car park here is a pay and display car park.

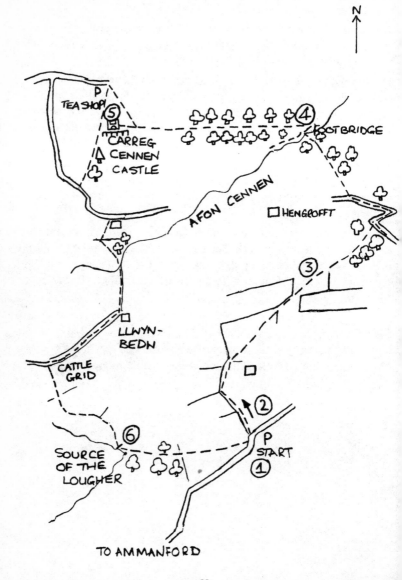

N

TEA SHOP

P

⑤

CARREG
CENNEN
CASTLE

④

FOOTBRIDGE

AFON CENNEN

☐ HENGROFFT

③

☐
LLWYN-
BEDN

CATTLE
GRID

②

⑥

P
START

①

SOURCE
OF THE
LOUGHER

TO AMMANFORD

82

Carreg Cennen Castle

A well marked, enjoyable ramble for all the family, including one of the most spectacular attractions in the National Park.

OS maps: 1:50 000: Swansea and Gower 159.

            1:25 000 Outdoor Leisure 12, The Brecon Beacons National Park Western and central area. (Note: This map doesn't cover the entire walk, ensure you keep the map from this book with you.)

Start: Roadside parking on the minor road which crosses the moors from the A4069 to the A483. GR673180.

Access: By car, the start can be reached by taking the minor road west from the A4069 across the moors towards Ammanford. Alternatively, approach the same road from the west, taking the A474 east from Ammanford and then turning left towards Cathilas before turning right and right again towards the open moors. It is also possible to approach from the north via the village of Trapp.

            NB It is possible to start the walk at Carreg Cennen itself. GR666194. The route is identical but the castle will be visited at either the start or the finish of the walk. By following the suggested route the castle will mark the half way point where the facilities of the tea shop etc. will be welcome.

Grade: Easy - The route follows good, well marked paths through a variety of woodland and farmland. There is a small, relatively gentle climb through the woods to the castle.

Points of Interest:

1. The area of open moorland south of the road is the western extremities of the Mynydd Du (or *Black Mountain*). (Not to be confused with the Black Mountains on the eastern side of the National Park.) This is the true wilderness area of the Brecon Beacons, designated a Site of Special Scientific Interest or SSSI.

The Black Mountain contains a fascinating mixture of geological features. In the west there are the huge sandstone ridges of the Carmarthen Fan, dropping hundreds of feet to open moorland below. Below these the glacial formed lakes of Llyn y Fan Fawr and Llyn y Fan Fach are contained by huge banks of debris (moraine) left by the receding glaciers and home to many myths and legends. Elsewhere there are limestone areas littered with shake holes, swallow holes and caves so typical of this landscape and home to many Alpine plants.

2. Just after leaving the road you will see, to your right, a strange lumpy area known as the pillow mounds. These are thought to be the remains of a bronze age burial site dating from around 3000BC. It is, however, possible that they are the remains of commercially farmed rabbit warrens, a common practice in Victorian times.

3. Before dropping down from the hilltop to the farmland below, you will get some of the best views of Carreg Cennen Castle perched on huge limestone cliffs on the other side of the valley.

4. The castle is surrounded by ancient woodland. As you cross the river Cennen and climb the hill it is predominantly oak whilst, to the south of the Castle, it is mainly ash. The woodlands are home to many species of bird. Look out for blue tits, marsh tits, long tailed tits and great tits as well as nuthatches, treecreepers and many types of warbler. If you sit still for long enough, the birds tend to carry on as if you weren't there. It can be fascinating watching the members of the tit family as they perform all types of gymnastics on tiny branches, seeking out insects to eat.

5. Carreg Cennen Castle, perched high above perilous limestone crags, is one of the most spectacular sights in the National Park. Almost fairy tale like from a distance, it offers huge views over the surrounding

area. The castle, as it is now, was built during the thirteenth century and, unlike the castles of North Wales, was probably built by the Welsh not the Normans. It did however change hands regularly in its early days and, despite its look of impregnability, had no fewer than ten owners in ten years during the latter part of the century. Its owners included Rhys ap Gruffudd, the Earl of Hereford and Sir John Gifford, who was responsible for many of the later modifications. In 1462, after the Wars of the Roses, and in the hands of the Yorkists, the castle became a den for local bandits and was eventually demolished to the condition it is now in. Local labour was cheap in those days, over five hundred men did the work and were paid a total of only £28 between them.

The site was occupied long before the castle was built. Roman coins dating to the first century indicate the earliest known activity. It is, however, difficult to imagine that earlier civilisations wouldn't have made use of its natural defences.

As a place to visit the castle is quite superb. There are many signs and information boards around the site explaining key features and much of the history. Allow a good hour to explore, although it would be easy to take a lot longer.

6. The limestone country around the castle is peppered with caves, many of which still house rivers and streams. The source of the river Loughor is typical. Reached by crossing a stile and scrambling over a fallen tree bridge, it is possible to see where the infant river rises from its cave before continuing on southwards towards Ammanford. Close by is an old lime kiln with a quarry behind. Although out of commission since the turn of the century, there are many kilns and quarries in the area, once an important part of local industry.

The Red Kite - A conservation success story

Whilst walking in the north and west of the National Park you may be lucky enough to see, what must be, Britain's most beautiful bird - the red kite (milvus milvus), which is now making a comeback in the area. The pleasure of watching its effortless, soaring flight is further enhanced by the knowledge that it was once on the brink of extinction in Britain and in these days of environmental disasters worldwide, it is encouraging to see a living success story.

Similar in size to the far more common buzzard, it is easily recognised by its slimmer, longer wings and distinctive long, forked tail. Its plumage is an extraordinary cocktail of russet red and chestnut brown with white patches on the underside of the wings. The head is a white-silver colour with a yellow bill. It literally hangs in the air, sometimes circling and can cover great distances in a very short time. Its call is a high pitched mew.

These birds have been actively hunted and destroyed since the middle ages, at one time there was even a bounty on their heads! By the beginning of this century there was only a handful left in the land, all congregated in the wild hills of mid Wales. Determined work by conservation groups such as the RSPB and English Nature, with the support of landowners, has seen the careful release of birds imported from Europe and 1992 saw the first successful breeding of the species in England and Scotland. This has halted the decline and the population is now growing and spreading out. These days the red kite is completely protected by law and it is illegal to harm or disturb the birds or their nests. There have even been armed guards in some areas! Sadly there is still some illegal persecution, with birds being poisoned or shot and eggs or young being stolen from nests. Should you ever witness any suspicious activity, it should be reported to the police immediately.

The birds feed on a wide variety of food which, as well as carrion includes small mammals, small birds, insects and even earthworms. Although normally seen hunting in areas of open moorland the red kite nests in trees, usually, in nests previously used by buzzards or crows. It will lay up to three eggs during April and will continue to feed the young until July. During this time it will be particularly busy providing food for its hungry family and can therefore be spotted more often. It is, however, incredibly shy and could be frightened into abandoning its nest just by seeing people nearby.

The "Kite Country Project" has been set up to provide information to the public on the red kite and its environment. It offers a number of locations where the birds can be observed both in the wild and at special feeding stations, there is also a Kite Country Exhibition at the Llandovery Heritage Centre on the north west boundary of the National Park. For information on the Kite Country Project, tel: 01686-624143.

Walk Directions: (-) denotes point of interest.

1. Start at the junction of a stony track with the minor road GR673180 (1). Take the stony track from the road in a northwesterly direction. Carry on along this path crossing two stiles then turning right into a field (2).

2. The path here is fairly clear. Cross the field and start to go down hill, where you will join up with a fence on your left. At the end of this go through a gate and carry on down to join another track on a hairpin bend (3).

3. Carry on along this new track for a hundred metres and around another hairpin bend, this time to the left. Immediately after this you will see a stile on your right with a sign to the castle.

4. Cross the stile and drop down the shady lane which will take you to the river Cennen. Cross two footbridges and two stiles.

5. After the second footbridge you will join a path crossing yours. Turn right onto this and then immediately sharp left and up the hill (4).

6. Carry straight on up the hill and eventually you will come to a gate. This is the entrance to the castle grounds where a small admission fee is paid. Turn left here and carry on to the castle itself (5).

7. When you have finished exploring, retrace your steps back to the gate and turn left to follow the lane down to the car park and tea shop.

8. After the tea shop and before you get to the car park, turn left through the buildings and follow a footpath along the side of a wood. After 300 metres rejoin the road and turn left.

9. Carry on along the road for 300 metres until you have almost reached a building on your right. Just before this building you should take a footpath on the right. Drop down through the fields crossing two stiles. You will then come to a footbridge over the river. Cross the

bridge and now go uphill, over a gate and up the side of the pasture to Llwyn Bedw farm.

10. Turn right and follow the track for about 800 metres. After fording a stream, go uphill and slightly to the right where you will come to a cattle grid. Here, turn left over a stile and across the field to reach a stream on your right and a small bridge.

11. Follow the course of the stream for approximately 500 metres and over two stiles. You will come to a small copse with a stile on your right (6). After visiting the source of the loughor, climb back over the stile and turn right, continuing past the lime kiln.

12. You will now come out into open pasture. Cross the stile and walk across the field to the far right hand corner. Here it joins the road, where you should see your car.

Facilities

In the small hamlet beneath the castle there is a tea shop open during the main season. There are public toilets in the castle car park.

This is a fairly remote area so it is worth carrying essentials such as food and water.

The nearby Castle Farm Rare Breeds Centre has a wide selection of rare agricultural animals to see, there is an admission charge.

The Mynydd Du - The Black Mountain

A big, wild walk over mainly pathless, open moorland, high mountains and a wonderful rocky gorge. This is a large undertaking, suited to experienced walkers with good map and compass skills. Route finding could prove difficult in poor visibility.

OS maps:	1:50 000 The Brecon Beacons 160:
	1:25 000 Outdoor Leisure 12, The Brecon Beacons National Park West and Central area.
Start:	Lay-by behind the Gwyn Arms public house at Glyntawe on the A4067, 8 kilometers north of Abercraf. GR 846166.
Access:	By car, follow the A4067 north west from its junction with the A4221. The lay-by and pub are on the right, half a kilometre further on than the car park for the Dan yr Ogof caves.
Grade:	Strenuous. This is a long walk over difficult terrain. There are a number of fairly stiff climbs and some sections are without a clear path to follow. This is a route for experienced walkers only. When in spate the Afon Haffes can be difficult to cross.

Points of Interest:

1. The Mynydd Du (or *The Black Mountain*) is the last true wilderness area in the National Park. It is a Site of Special Scientific Interest or SSSI and is home to many birds, animals and rare plant life. The land west of Fan Hir is now owned by the National Park Authority who are committed to maintaining its unique landscape. There are few clear paths and very little trace of human activity, which adds to the whole wilderness experience.

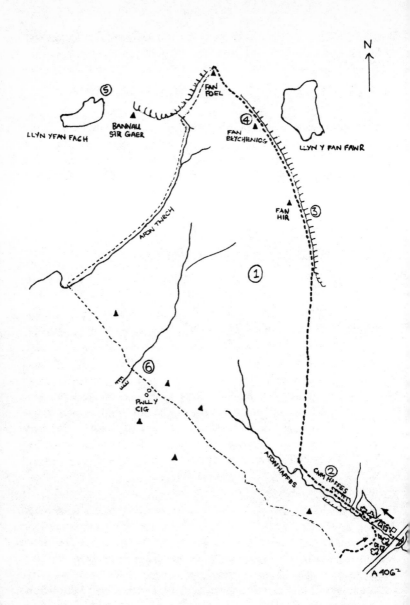

LLYN YFAN FACH

⑤

BANNAU
SIR GAER

FAN
FOEL

④

FAN
BRYCHEINIOG

LLYN Y FAN FAWR

AFON TWRCH

FAN
HIR

③

①

⑥

PWLL Y
CIG

AFON HAFFES

CWM HAFFES

②

A 4067

N
↑

2. Cwm Haffes is a spectacular, rocky gorge. The Afon Haffes plunges down two hundred vertical metres in less than two kilometres from the peaty moorland above. The area is littered with huge boulders which are debris from the glacial melt. At times the river literally gushes through narrow gaps in the huge red sandstone slabs that make up its bed. There are many naturally formed "hanging gardens" made up of ferns and lichen, often crowned with the beautiful red berries of the rowan tree or mountain ash.

Kestrels and buzzards are often seen here hunting for the small birds and mammals that make the cwm their home.

3. There are few adjectives that adequately describe the spectacular airy ridges of Fan Hir, Fan Brycheiniog and Fan Foel. Shaped into a huge scarp by the retreating of the Ice Age, they stand proudly over two hundred metres above the moors below. In places, huge slabs overhang the cliffs like stone gang planks. Standing on these slabs gives a feeling of spaciousness and offers wonderful photograph opportunities.

4. Fan Brycheiniog is the highest mountain in the Mynydd Du at 802m (2,630 ft). On its summit, next to the trig point is a huge stone windbreak. The wind certainly accelerates over the ridge and this offers a great place to take a rest and get some refreshment. This area is often referred to as the Horns of the Mynydd Du, getting its name from the likeness between the scarp edge and a horn, a likeness which isn't all that obvious. Bannau Brycheiniog actually translates into the Beacons of Breckonshire whilst to your west, Bannau Shir Gâr is the Beacons of Carmarthenshire. You may deduce, therefore, that the boundary runs between the two summits. It, in fact, follows the path of the Afon Twrch, as does the next stage of the walk.

On a clear day the views from the summit stretch for miles and it is possible to see the whole of the northern edge of the National Park. The twin peaks of Pen y Fan and Corn Du stand proudly to the east whilst, further on, the ridges of the Black Mountains slope down towards the river Wye. Further north are the mountains of the Elan Valley and, in the distance it is possible to see Cader Idris on the North Wales Coast. To the west, the Pembrokeshire coast can often be seen.

5. Directly below the ridge is Llyn y Fan Fawr, a glacial lake and one of two that can be seen on this walk. The other, visible from the ridge after Fan Foel, is Llyn y Fan Fach. The "magic lake" as it is often called is the subject of a legend regarding a lady of the lake and a local shepherd boy. The lady appeared from the lake and bewitched the boy, who's name was Rhiwallon. He fell for her beauty and asked her to marry him. She agreed and they wed on the one condition that he should never strike her with iron.

She possessed many magic skills and potions which she passed on to her eldest son, named Rhiwallon after his father. Eventually he did strike her and, true to her word, she left him and returned to the lake taking all their possessions with her. The son went on to become a famous healer, passing his skills on to others and giving rise to a line of local healers who became known as the Physicians of Myddfai.

Whilst initially sounding rather far fetched it is thought by many that the story goes back to the arrival of the Iron Age in Wales. The lady may have been from Bronze Age people living in the area which would explain her fear of Iron. Her people would have had knowledge of herbal medicine which would explain her special healing powers and Myddfai was indeed home to a line of doctors, going back over six hundred years. Perhaps it is from stories like this that many legends are born.

6. Having crossed the county boundary and the Afon Twrch for the last time you now enter an unusual limestone landscape, probably the most extreme example of this in the National Park. The river Twrch, incidentally, is named after a magic Boar in yet another legend. You will notice on the map that this area is littered with swallow holes, shake holes, caves and limestone outcrops. This is typical of a carboniferous limestone landscape. The acidic rain literally dissolves the rock in places, forming caves which then carry rivers and streams underground. Further erosion above forms holes and craters in the ground and gives the whole area a look that resembles the surface of the moon. Many cavers and pot holers visit this area, in order to explore the massive labyrinth of tunnels below. On the surface, strange limestone outcrops can be seen, almost pavement like in places. This area is the subject of the Glyn Tawe Geology Trail starting from

nearby Craig-y-nos Country Park.

Walk Directions: (-) denotes point of interest.

1. Where the Afon Haffes crosses the lay-by take the footpath up its right hand side heading upstream towards the main road. Cross the road and over a stile following the path up past a house and along the edge of a small copse before reaching the river.

2. (1)Your objective is to walk up the river. It is normally easier to start off by fording here and keeping to the left hand bank as much as possible. You may need to cross the stream a few times in order to stay on the best paths. After about one kilometre you will come to a waterfall. Pass this on the right hand bank and shortly afterwards you will emerge from the gorge onto open moorland.

3. Once onto the open moorland the river starts to form an oxbow lake. From here your objective is to head due north, following whatever tracks you can find. Eventually you will make out the narrow spur of the Fan Hir ridge in front of you.

4. Aim to the right of this spur and you will join the main ridge path coming up from your right (2). Turn left and follow the ridge for 6 glorious kilometres over the summits of Fan Hir, Fan Brycheiniog (3) and Fan Foel.

5. After Fan Foel the ridge turns south west (4) and begins to drop into a saddle (5) before the huge climb up to Bannau Shir Gâr. Relax, you don't have to climb this. Instead, head up the stream for approximately 50 metres. Here, on your right, is the start of another stream. Although it is often dry, it is easily recognisable by its steep banks. This stream heads first south west and then due south to join the Afon Twrch and run along the county boundary. There are a number of small paths which follow the stream down the valley at various heights. Take one of these and follow the stream for 2 kilometres.

6. At GR802197 the stream deviates from its south westerly course for the first time by turning first right (north west) for 200 metres and then left (south west) creating a small oxbow lake. Here, marked on the

map, there is a public bridleway which is sadly no longer clear. The route however, follows the course of this bridleway so you need to cross the stream at the right hand bend of the river and follow a bearing of 150 degrees magnetic up the hill the other side. Keep to the right of the two hills you will see (6). After 800 metres you will reach the top of this hill and around here it is possible to pick up one of many faint paths which head back down the hill to Pwll y Cig.

7. Ford the stream at GR811185 where once again there is a clear path heading up hill in a south westerly direction. Take this path passing a small pond on your right after 300 metres.

8. The navigation again becomes straightforward now as you follow this path through small limestone outcrops and past many areas of shakeholes for the next 3 kilometres, keeping all the time to the main track.

9. The path splits left and right at Twyn Spratt. Take the right fork which takes you down to a wall. Turn left and follow the track along the wall for 500 metres back to the Afon Haffes which you cross to join the track you started on. From the small gate retrace your steps past the farmhouse and across the road to your car.

Facilities

This is an isolated area and you will need to be self sufficient. There is, however, a payphone in the pub.

Dan-yr-ogof Showcaves - Underground show caves, a museum, Dinosaur Park and Shire Horse Centre. Open from Easter to October. Situated only minutes from the start of the walk.

Craig-y-nos Country Park - Situated a couple of miles south of the start of the walk. As well as information, displays and events the park is set in over 40 acres of woodland and meadow and would make a great day out for the family.

Other Information

Youth Hostels

There are six Youth Hostels in and around the National Park, some are quite small and advanced booking is well recommended.

Bryn Poeth Uchaf : Hafod-y-Pant, Cynghordy, Llandovery. SA20 0NB
01550 750235

Capel-y-Ffin: Abergavenny. NP7 7NP
01873 890650

Llanddeusant: The Old Red Lion, Llanddeusant, Llangadog.
SA19 6UL
01550 740619

Llwyn-y-Celyn: Libanus, Brecon. LD3 8NH
01874 624261

Ty'n-y-Caeau (Nr Brecon): Groesffordd, Brecon. LD3 7SW
01874 665270

Ystradfellte: Tai'r Heol, Ystradfellte, Aberdare. CF44 9JF
01639 720301

Walks with History

If you want to experience the very best of Wales, then these are the books for you. The walks are graded and there is something for everybody – short walks for families and more demanding routes to satisfy even the most experienced hillwalker.

Walks on the Llŷn Peninsula
PART 1 - SOUTH & WEST – N Burras & J. Stiff.
ISBN 0-86381-343-7; **£4.50**
This series combines walks with history, stories and legends. Pastoral walks as well as coastal & mountain panoramas.

Walks on the Llŷn Peninsula
PART 2 - NORTH & EAST – N. Burras & J. Stiff.
ISBN 0-86381-365-8: **£4.50**

Walks in the Snowdonia Mountains
– Don Hinson. 45 walks, mostly circular, 96 pages, inc. accurate maps and drawings. 96pp ISBN 0-86381-385-2; New Edition: **£3.75**

Walks in North Snowdonia
– Don Hinson. 100km of paths to help those wishing to explore the area further. 96pp ISBN 0-86381-386-0; New Edition; **£3.75**

New Walks in Snowdonia
– Don Hinson. 43 circular walks together with many variations. This book introduces you to lesser known paths and places which guide book writers seem to have neglected. Maps with every walk. Pen & ink drawings.
96pp ISBN 0-86381-390-9; New Edition; **£3.75**

Circular Walks in North Pembrokeshire
– Paul Williams, 14 walks, 112 pages. ISBN 0-86381-420-4; **£4.50**

Circular Walks in South Pembrokeshire
– Paul Williams, 14 walks, 120 pages. ISBN 0-86381-421-2; **£4.50**

From Mountain Tops to Valley Floors
Salter & Worral. ISBN 0-86381-430-1; **£4.50**
Detailed information for casual/family walks and for the more adventurous walker.

NEW FOR 1998:
Circular Walks in the Brecon Beacons National Park;
ISBN 0-86381-476-X; **£4.50**
Circular Walks on Anglesey; ISBN 0-86381-478-6; **£4.50**
Circular Walks in Gower; ISBN 0-86381-479-4; **£4.50**
Circular Walks in Central Wales; ISBN 0-86381-480-8; **£4.50**
Circular Walks in Gwent; ISBN 0-86381-477-8; **£4.50**